CU00923897

History from the Sources
General Editor: John Morris

ARTHURIAN PERIOD SOURCES
VOL. 5

ARTHURIAN SOURCES

Vol. 5
Genealogies and Texts

ARTHURIAN PERIOD SOURCES

1 **Arthurian Sources, Vol. 1**, by John Morris
   Introduction, Notes and Index
      How to use *Arthurian Sources*; Introduction and Notes;
      Index to *The Age of Arthur*

2 **Arthurian Sources, Vol. 2**, by John Morris
   *Annals (**A**) and Charters (**C**)*

3 **Arthurian Sources, Vol. 3**, by John Morris
   Persons
      Ecclesiastics (**E**) (alphabetically listed)
      Laypeople (**L**) (alphabetically listed)

4 **Arthurian Sources, Vol. 4**, by John Morris
   *Places and Peoples (**P**), and Saxon Archaeology (**S**)*
      Places and Peoples (alphabetically listed)
      Saxon Archaeology:
         The Chronology of Early Anglo-Saxon Archaeology;
         Anglo-Saxon Surrey; The Anglo-Saxons in Bedfordshire

5 **Arthurian Sources, Vol. 5**, by John Morris
   *Genealogies (**G**) and Texts (**T**)*
      Genealogies
         Editions by Egerton Phillimore (1856-1937): *The Annales Cambriae*
         and Old-Welsh Genealogies from B.L. MS. Harley 3859; Pedigrees
         from Jesus College (Oxford) MS. 20; Bonedd y Saint from N.L.W.
         MS. Peniarth 12
      Texts discussed
         Gospel-books; Honorius's Letter; Laws; Martyrologies; Muirchú's
         Life of St. Patrick; *Notitia Dignitatum*; *Periplus*; Ptolemy; The 'Tribal
         Hidage'; Welsh Poems

6 **Arthurian Sources, Vol. 6**, by John Morris
   Studies in Dark-Age History
      Celtic Saints—a Note; Pelagian Literature; Dark Age Dates; The Dates
      of the Celtic Saints; The Date of Saint Alban; Christianity in Britain,
      300-700—the Literary Evidence; Studies in the Early British Church—a
      Review; Gildas

7 **Gildas**, edited and translated by Michael Winterbottom
      The Ruin of Britain; Fragments of Lost Letters; Penitential or Monastic
      Rule

8 **Nennius**, edited and translated by John Morris
      'Select Documents on British History'; The Welsh Annals

9 **St. Patrick**, edited and translated by A.B.E. Hood
      Declaration; Letter to Coroticus; Sayings; Muirchú's Life of St. Patrick

ARTHURIAN SOURCES

Vol. 5
Genealogies and Texts

JOHN MORRIS

PHILLIMORE

1995

Published by
PHILLIMORE & CO. LTD.
Shopwyke Manor Barn, Chichester, Sussex

ISBN 0 85033 763 1

Printed and bound in Great Britain by
HARTNOLLS LTD.
Bodmin, Cornwall

CONTENTS

GENEALOGIES

GENEALOGIES

Later ages have preserved the genealogies of very many local rulers in the British Isles in the Arthurian period. They connect the people whom they name with one another and with particular regions, but their historical value is limited unless the dates can be ascertained from other texts. Fortunately, a high proportion of the names occur in other sources, principally Annals and Saints' Lives. The dates of successive names frequently match, but sometimes they do not. The many minor problems so occasioned cannot be resolved without understanding of the genealogist's purpose, and of the nature of the errors to which he was prone.

The genealogist's business was practical. He was required to link his living patron with heroes and princes of the past, whose names were well known in his own day, not to connect them with made-up names. Normally, the two ends of his pedigree are sound; what he invented or manipulated are the links which connect them. The nature of his trade demanded different techniques in different countries. The British pedigrees are in the main convergent. Their business is to show that great kings, from Hywel Dda in the tenth century to Henry VII in the fifteenth, were legitimate heirs by inheritance and descent of the several dynasties of many parts of Britain. Since men can have but one father apiece, they must inherit other kingdoms through their mothers, and the structure of the later Welsh pedigrees turns upon contriving marriages between heiresses of known dynasties and ancestors of the patron. Their style is clearly illustrated in the contrast between the Harleian and Jesus College collections, discussed below (**GB**). A collection of pedigrees compiled about A.D. 800, perhaps on the basis of an earlier collection 200 years older, forms the substance of the Harleian text, which is essentially a collection of local traditions, unrelated to one another. The Jesus text, in its final form a work of the thirteenth century, drawing on a tenth-century version, adds the links which made Hywel (died 950) and his son heirs to all their predecessors, and Llewelyn the Great (died 1240) heir to all Hywel's descendants. Naturally, many of the marriages are between people who lived many generations apart. Any calculations of date based on marriages are likely to be wrong; but the substantive dynasties thus artificially connected derive from a much older and sounder tradition.

The Irish genealogies are divergent. These had to show that very many local lords were direct male descendants of great kings. Marriages have little to do with the structure. The Irish technique is to credit the great name with a very large number of sons, and to tack many local dynasties on to them. Niall of the Nine Hostages has dozens of sons and scores of grandsons. The technique is continued for later generations. Some two dozen names are tacked on to the mid-seventh-century descendants of his grandson Énda mac Loegairi. The practice is very frequent. It therefore follows that the younger sons of kings, when they are not attested outside the genealogies, are likely to be mechanical devices, their dates as well as their parentage at fault. In the main, the English lists follow the Irish model: Ida and Aethelfrith are equipped with sons on an Irish scale, and, although the extant lists of descendants are preserved for only a few of them, the sons remain as the stumps of lost pedigrees, their form Irish. Sometimes, a half-truth lies behind the tacking: the hereditary claim of Coenwulf of Mercia, died 821, is substantiated by turning his alleged ancestor Cenwalh from Penda's brother-in-law to Penda's brother. The differences between two Dal Riada texts of c. 650 and c. 700, both of which survive in their original form, give a clear instance of how genealogical tradition grew and changed.

The legends of the saints also disturbed tradition. Several notable saints were of royal birth. Columba was a prince of Uí Néill, high kings of Ireland; several English kings abdicated their thrones, from motives of piety and not of compulsion, to become monks and abbots. A large number of English queens and princesses entered monasteries, and so did several seventh-century Frankish queens and high court-officials. It became a fashionable convention of the hagiographer that a saint should have royal parents, and very many saints were tacked onto dynasties, in Ireland and in Wales, especially by the writers of the eighth and ninth centuries. Two works devoted to saints' parentage have particularly influenced later genealogists, the Irish Tract on the *Mothers of the Saints*, attributed to Angus the Culdee, and the Welsh *Bonedd y Saint*, mainly concerned with both fathers and mothers. Sometimes the saint is made the son of a known queen as well as of a known king, but more often his mother was named in earlier tradition and made to marry a king; and sometimes a poorly contrived pedigree, with its generations far too few, or far too many, links the saint with the king. All such connections have to be disregarded, and no attempt can be made to date a pedigree from the saint attached to it. But, as with the secular genealogist, the kings to whom they are attached are real, or were believed to be real when the work was written. *Bonedd y Saint* in particular preserves a whole number of local pedigrees which have not otherwise survived; since, when it depends on pedigrees known elsewhere, it accurately reports the main tradition of other genealogists, the unrecorded lists which it reproduces are likely to be equally valid, apart from their connection with the saint concerned.

In addition to these specific sources of error, the genealogical collections were subject to the normal accidents of transmission: they leave out names, duplicate others, misunderstand, misdate, or make wrong equations between people of the same name. These textual problems however are common to the transmission of most ancient texts, and are for the most part soluble, when different manuscripts are collated, and the reasons for the errors thereby made plain. Each country, and each text, also has its own minor problems, discussed below.

Most genealogists worked with existing manuscripts, adapting their texts to link the men of his own day with those there recorded. The compilers invented only when they had to. Several texts show how they worked when they had no information. The British lists carrying the ancestry of their heroes back beyond the later fourth century follow two main patterns. One takes a list of known Roman emperors, turns them to a father-to-son succession, and fills in a few names taken from lists whose context the genealogist did not know, to bridge the gap between the sons of Constantine or Magnus Maximus and the first attested native names. Usually these scrappy bridging lists are meaningless, but one seems to have been a pedigree of the Belgic kings of the century before the Roman conquest in A.D. 43; since no popular memory of these kings survived, it is likely to have come from a manuscript source, probably a lost Roman history. The second form is to indicate time, and fill in about the right number of generations between the late fourth century and the time of Beli Mawr (Cunobelinus) and of Christ, a synchronism achieved by marrying Beli to a cousin of the Virgin Mary. A number of these names are geographical, Dimet, Dobun, Dumn, Ceint, etc., for the tribal names Demetae, Dobunni, Dumnonii, Cantii etc., and their probable origin is a text which linked personal names with places, misunderstood or adapted. The required number of generations is obtained by doubling the names, writing Dum son of Guordumn etc., in the manner of the early Pictish king-lists.

The nature of Irish pedigrees, where information was not to hand, may be seen in the schemes for the fourth and earlier centuries for Uí Néill, the Eoganacht, and the Ulaid. The genealogists, like the Annalists, had before them a reasonably consistent account of the dynasty of Niall's ancestors, stretching back to the second century A.D., but their traditions about other dynasties and other provinces are utterly inconsistent, both internally and in their relations with the main dynasty. It is abundantly clear that, when the genealogist had no texts before him, he turned to the romances, where poets related legendary heroes to each other without bothering to heed whether they were contemporaries or lived centuries apart. The instances of how the genealogists behaved when they had to invent are in sharp contrast with their accounts of later centuries. The influence of romance is rarely apparent, save in the marriages of a few Irish kings; the numerous different pedigrees are internally consistent, and they also place in the same generation large numbers of people from different kingdoms whom the Annals bring together in time. The confusions of earlier centuries emphasise the solid consistency of the tradition from the fifth century onward. Similarly, the West Saxon lists show how English genealogists worked when they had no information and were compelled to invent, and the manipulations of the sixth-century Northumbrian records show how they rearranged material. Since these texts enable us to see how they invented and adapted, we have to recognise the existence of unadulterated early tradition in the rest of the texts which have no signs of such doctoring.

It is normally possible to separate contrivance from the bulk of the texts, which derive from earlier originals without deliberate alteration. But the best of the genealogies are undated, and few have dates supplied from other sources for more than scattered individuals. The principal factual control is that human biology has not changed. Men reached maturity and begot children at roughly the same sort of ages as in other societies. Few men become fathers before they are 18 or 20; relatively few children are born when the fathers are over about 45. The great majority are born when their fathers are between 20 and 40, and a rough and ready rule-of-thumb average of 30 years to a generation is a valid yardstick of most lists over a long period.

But it is a yardstick which must be used with sense and caution. It is obvious that when a man has many children, he is likely to beget the eldest when he is 20, to be 40 when the youngest is born. If early children recur for two or three generations in one line, late born in another, second cousins will be a generation apart: in 120 years it is possible in quite normal circumstances to have six, four or three generations, but rarely two or eight. Reckoning by 30 years to a generation is therefore a dubious guide unless there are frequent check-points. It tends in practice to work out over a long period, but to mislead in detail within that period. An obvious and simple example is the British royal family over the last two centuries, set out below with generation-intervals to the left of the names, the year denoting a time when the individual was in the prime of life:

1770	George III	1760-1820
1800	Edward, Duke of Kent	b.1767, d.1820
1830	Victoria	1837-1901
1860	Edward VII	1901-1910
1890	George V	1910-1936
1920	George VI	1937-1952
1950	Elizabeth II	1952-

The generation-intervals are not a bad guide to ages, but they are a poor guide to reigns. Two very long reigns are set against several shorter and against a younger son who never reigned. If the generation-years were our only guide to the events of each reign, the events connected with Edward VII, the Entente Cordiale or Bleriot's first flight across the Channel, would be dated 20 to 50 years too early, and the rise of Hitler would be dated 1890 × 1920.

Calculation by generations is therefore a very rough guide, unless checked by absolute dates at both ends. Fortunately, very many of the pedigrees here studied have such date-checks, and the known dates are therefore printed against the names. Several lines are continued beyond the seventh century, and the later control-dates may be seen. Often, these dates show that, in a particular case, the interval is longer or shorter than 30 years, and, when this happens, the generation-years shown are adjusted to fit the facts, thereby giving a closer guide to the date of the names placed between the fixed points.

In addition to these general considerations, each kind of genealogy had its own problems. Irish family nomenclature changed. The older form, *maqi mucoi* on inscriptions, for Adomnán (*c.* 700) regularly *moccu*, latinised as *gente*, meaning of the family of, normally relating to a people, dropped from use in the eighth century, and was commonly spelt *maccu*, confused with *mac*, son of. The dynasties used *aui*, on inscriptions, *Uí* in texts; *nepotes*, Adomnán, strictly used by him in contrast to the *moccu* of their plebeian subjects. As distinctions blurred, and the genealogists connected more and more local families to great dynasties, men became *mac ua*, in Latin *filius nepotum*; and later copyists failed to understand. Confusion is sometimes easy to detect, especially with names beginning with a vowel. 'Mac Cuansi' is plainly 'maccu An(d)si'; the descendants of (Colla) Uais, 'maccu Uais' were read as Mac Cuais, and 'Uí Mac Cuais' became his supposed dynastic descendants. Ultán mac Huí Cunga in *AT*, *FM*, *CS* (cf. *AC*) is Ultán mac Caunga in AU 644. The net result of the confusion (discussed especially MacNeill, *PIRA*, 29 C, 1911-12, 59 ff.; cf. *Ériu*, 3, 1907, 42 ff, cf. 9, 1921-23, 55) was that the name of a man's father and of the founder of his dynasty were easily confused. A 'Cormac mac uí Cairpri' easily became a 'Cormac mac Cairpri', particularly in the fifth-century genealogical notes in the Annals. Similarly, confusion dropped the *mac* in the names of dynastic founders. Irish recorded names do not include persons with two personal names, although many men have a name and an epithet. But Niall's two grandsons, both named Conall, sons of Crimthann and of Gulban, are distinguished as Conall Crimthann and Conall Gulban, the *mac* preserved only in *AI*, leading the unwary to suppose one person instead of two.

The Welsh had no such problem. But their records begin with the establishment of large realms on Roman authority, subsequently subdivided. Magnus Maximus and Cunedda are equipped with many sons, several of whom name districts. It is extremely probable that these were in origin Maximus' nominees and Cunedda's subordinate generals, turned by genealogical convention into his sons, since he was the source of their authority. The practical difference is that they are to be seen as contemporaries of Maximus, or of Cunedda and his actual sons, not as persons who ruled a generation later. These are among the principal considerations which govern the grammar of the criticism of genealogies.

The genealogies exist in very many manuscripts. The Welsh lists were continued in the medieval and post-Renaissance centuries, when they became divergent, serving as the starting point for pedigrees of local notables, many versions being embellished by antiquarian fancy. The Irish collections, in a number of extensive collections, contain a large number of lines terminating about the early tenth century, but many were continued into later centuries. They tend to keep distinct the texts relating to the Mythological Cycle, of the centuries B.C., to the Conchobar Cycle, of the time of Augustus and Christ, to the Finn Cycle of about the third century B.C., to the Historical Cycle of the fifth to seventh centuries A.D., and to the well recorded kings of the seventh to tenth centuries.

Since the collections vary in detail, the tradition which they record cannot be reconstructed from any single text. The manuscripts need to be collated. To isolate the earlier tradition from later adaptation, it is necessary to select those texts least subject to later manipulation. The texts used for the collated genealogies printed below are the following.

IRISH (GI)

CGH M.A. O'Brien, *Corpus Genealogiarum Hiberniae*, Vol. 1, Dublin, 1962, which indexes some 13,000 persons, few of them later than the eleventh century, and draws on the large collection in MS. Rawlinson B.502, on the Book of Leinster genealogies, collating the variants to the pedigrees there contained found in the Books of Lecan and Ballymote. The system of reference employed in *CGH* is to distinguish each pedigree by the folio and line in which it begins in R (Rawlinson) or LL (Book of Leinster). Since *CGH* has few Connacht pedigrees, I have used *O'C*, The O'Clery Genealogies, *Analecta Hibernica* 18, 1951, which contains over 2,000 pedigrees of pre-Norman families, without an index, each number from 1 onwards. These genealogies can often also be found in the Mac Firbis, Laud, Keating, and other collections; where they differ from *CGH*, the difference is usually due to antiquarian speculation rather than to greater knowledge of early tradition. The genealogical notes in the Annals usually derive from the main tradition but often include lists not there preserved; these notes are subject to the same sources of error as the genealogies. In the earlier Annals there is a tendency to preserve the father's name, but not his further ancestors.

BRITISH (GB)

BGG *Bonedd Gwyr y Gogledd* (Genealogies of the Men of the North), printed in *TYP*, Appendix II, p. 238, and in *FAB* 2, 454, both from NLW MS. Peniarth 45, formerly Hengwrt 536, almost without differences. The numbering of the entries by the modern editors differs. The entry on the unity of the Kynver-chyn, Kynnvydyon and Coeling is included under number 6 in *FAB*, separately numbered as 7 in *TYP*, so that *FAB* 7-12 = *TYP* 8- 13; the numbering of *TYP* is here adopted. The entries are all fifth- and sixth-century; but the second group, 8-13, has been extensively, though clumsily, manipulated in the interests of the Alclud kings at a substantially later date.

H *Harley* MS. 3859 includes a text of Nennius, of the *Annales Cambriae*, and 31 genealogies, printed *YC* 9, 1888, 169 ff. (see below, pp. 13-55). The *Annales* end in 954, though blank years continue to 973, the genealogies are substantially of about 800, the first two extended to Owain son of Hywel Dda, who came to the throne in 950.

J Jesus College MS., 20 pedigrees reproduce those of *H*, omitting some and adding others which appear to derive from the same source as *H*, and extend the lists in two stages, through Rhodri Mawr (died 877) to Hywel Dda (died 950), and then to the thirteenth century, linking the lines by marriages, often plainly devised. See below, pp. 56-65, for the text.

N *Nennius* (cf. under *English* below) contains some British pedigrees.

ByS *Bonedd y Saint* (Genealogies of the Saints) printed *VSBG*, 320 ff. from 8 MSS. (listed p.xvii), the last of which, previously printed in *RC*, 50, 1933, 363 ff. contain a few items not reproduced in *VSBG*. The tract attaches saints of the sixth and seventh centuries to pedigrees of persons believed to have ruled the localities where the saints were venerated, or were held to have been born, in those centuries. The statement that 'the tract was compiled in the twelfth century' is a guess, based primarily on the fact that the earliest MSS. are extant are of the thirteenth and on an assumption that the tract is likely to have had somthing to do with Bishop Bernard of St Davids. The date is a not unreasonable guess for the surviving text, since the twelfth century was a time of markedly revived interest in Saints' Lives, when Ricemarch, Lifris and others rewrote Lives from antiquated and ill preserved texts. But the text makes little of twelfth-century cults, save that it names David first among the descendants of Cunedda and shows signs of organic growth. Its order, like *H* and *J*, is geographical, starting with the Cunedda dynasty, the north, Armorica, the Cornovii, then two detached items, and Powys. Thereafter come a series of detached items which look like additions to the original. It is likely that the text rests upon a base substantially earlier than the twelfth century. The relationship of the saints to the dynasties is the invented element.

ARMORICA (Brittany) (**GA**)

CC *Comites Cornubiae*, from the Landevennec, Quimper and Quimperlé cartularies.

I *Iudoc* and

W *Winnoc* refer to the genealogies appended to the Lives of these Saints.

Brittany has no comprehensive collection of genealogies. These texts are supplemented by the contemporary notices of Gregory of Tours and by a number of Saints' Lives. The revival of hagiography in Brittany was centred in the time of the powerful ninth-century kings, Nominoi and Salomon, three centuries earlier than in Wales. A number of hagiographers were able to consult texts of the sixth and seventh centuries, whose orthography they reproduce. Although their information is less, what there is derives from a considerably older and stronger tradition than the Welsh. A few notices in the British lists, notably in *ByS* and in the texts which concern the Cornovii, also relate to Brittany.

ENGLISH (**GE**)

ASC The *Anglo-Saxon Chronicle* (ASC) contains a number of pedigrees, many dated
     to the ninth century, inserted against the names of kings, usually on their
     succession, in the manner of the genealogical entries in the Irish Annals.
B   *Bede, HE*, gives a very few genealogies, but meticulously explains the relation-
     ship of many rulers to their predecessors and contemporaries.
F   *Florence* of Worcester's Chronicle (1117) concludes with a collection of gen-
     ealogies in an appendix. A number of the relationships not found in ASC
     and Bede may be intelligent guesses based on their date, but there are
     also a number of names not there contained. Some of the relationships are
     improbable, but the names are unlikely to be Florence's invention. Some
     additional information is contained in the chronicles of his contemporaries.
     Symeon of Durham (SD) (1108), William of Malmesbury (W) (1120), and
     Henry of Huntingdon (H) (1130). Their chronicles are works of serious
     intent, wholly unlike the spoof history of their contemporary Geoffrey of
     Monmouth.
N   *Nennius* had a genealogical appendix containing two separate Bernician
     genealogies (57; 61b-65), both equipped with historical notes, both ending in
     the reign of Aldfrith (685-705); between them are placed genealogies of Kent
     (*c.* 670), East Anglia (*c.* 730), Mercia (796) and of a minor Deiran line
     (*c.* 800) with the descent of archbishop Egbert (died 766) from Ida. The
     northern portion of the text has been discussed by Jackson, in *Celt and Saxon*,
     ed. N. K. Chadwick, 21 ff. The whole is evidently a composite document, its
     first layer in Aldfrith's time, its latest *c.* 800. It contains one king, Aethelric
     of East Anglia, *c.* 730, not known to the English sources.
T   *The Oldest English Texts*, ed. Henry Sweet, 1885, contains a collection of
     pedigrees (*c.* 800). There was evidently an eighth-century English collection
     comparable with the Welsh, of which fragments have survived with additions
     to *c.* 800.

SCOTLAND

Picts have no genealogies, since fathers were not succeeded by sons. Their record
is in the form of a king-list.

Scots of Dal Riada in Argyle were Irish emigrants. The bulk of their record is Irish,
but it includes two local texts of high antiquity, the *Senchus Fer nAlban* of *c.*650 and
the 'Four chief *cenéla*' of *c.* 700. The numerous pedigrees of medieval Scotland are
almost entirely antiquarian fancies embroidered on an Irish base, adding nothing
to its historical record.

There are many genealogies which I have not been able to consult, either because they are unpublished, or because they are difficult of access. Although most of them are in varying degrees disturbed by antiquarian alteration, they are likely to explain some problems of detail and correct some of the inferences based on the texts here used, particularly in some of the Irish dynasties. The firm conclusion to be drawn from these texts is that they are subject to the ordinary processes of historical criticism. Almost all the problems of moment which they pose are capable of solution. It follows that there is an answer to each problem, and the evidence is normally sufficient to permit an interpretation. The Genealogies, the Annals, and the Saints' Lives offer few serious contradictions to each other, once the specific sources of error normal to each are detected and isolated.

EDITIONS OF *ANNALES CAMBRIAE* AND WELSH GENEALOGIES

by

Egerton Phillimore

(1856–1937)

THE

ANNALES CAMBRIÆ AND OLD-WELSH GENEALOGIES

FROM *HARLEIAN MS.* 3859.*

(LONDON, BRITISH LIBRARY, MS. HARLEY 3859)

OF the scanty existing remains of Old-Welsh, the only one
of any extent still remaining unpublished in any form available to scholars or students[1] consists of the early Welsh
Genealogies, embracing most of the royal and princely lines
of the Cymric race, immediately appended to the oldest
known Welsh annals, the *Annales Cambriæ*, in *Harleian MS.*
No. 3859. These Genealogies are now for the first time com-

---

[1] The whole Genealogies, with the annexed *Catalogue of Cities*, were
transcribed by (or for ?) the late Sir Samuel R. Meyrick, and printed by
him, with a partial translation, in the *Cambrian Quarterly Magazine* for
1832 (vol. iv, pp. 16—24). Of this performance we can only say (from
our own collation of it) that the number of the proper names
occurring in the text is *at least* exceeded by the number of mistakes
in its "reproduction". So incompetent was the transcriber, that
he read the concluding word of the MS. of "Nennius", of which
the Genealogies form part, which is simply *Amen*, as "αλλεχι, or
something very like it"! The first two Genealogies (those of Owain
ab Hywel Dda) are tolerably reproduced in the Preface to Aneurin
Owen's *Ancient Laws and Institutes of Wales* (1841), and (taken
thence) in that of the printed *Annales Cambriæ;* and so many of
the Genealogies as relate to the princely lines of Cumbria have also
been printed (with but few mistakes) by Skene in his *Chronicles of
the Picts, Chronicles of the Scots*, etc. (1867), pp. 15, 16, where they
follow extracts from the *Saxon Genealogies* and *Annales Cambriæ*,
also taken from *Harl.* 3859.

* Reprinted from *Y Cymmrodor* 9 (1888) 141–183

pletely and exactly reproduced from the unique[1] copy of them contained in that MS.

It has also been thought desirable to take the opportunity of simultaneously reproducing here the *Annales Cambriæ*, especially as in the printed editions of them (1) in *Monumenta Historica Britannica* (1848), p. 830, and (2) (taken thence) in the separate work to which they furnish the title, printed for the Master of the Rolls in 1860, they have been so amalgamated with two much later Chronicles (only to a limited extent copied from the earlier record) that the real nature and value of the older document are much obscured by the process. Amongst other reasons for printing the *Annales* and the Genealogies *together* are, that the former as well as the latter document is only found in this one MS.; that they were both compiled (as we shall see) at the same period, and very probably by the same person; and that, being both largely concerned with the same historical personages and events, they extensively illustrate one another. It may be added that the printed work, though in substance very accurate, makes no pretence to give in any way an *exact* transcription of our MS., and that we are here concerned with a MS. in which minute exactness of reproduction is of unusual importance. Not only is it expedient, both from the palæographical and from the historical point of view, to show the *precise* shape in which the' ancient Cymry kept their national records, but, from the philological point of view, a mere consideration of the mistakes of the MS. will suffice to guide anyone to the important conclusion that its transcriber (if not also the transcriber of *his*

---

[1] Some of the identical genealogies occur in a modernised form, and with important variations, in the collection of the fourteenth century contained in No. 20 of the MSS. at Jesus College, Oxford, recently printed by us in *Y Cymmrodor*, vol. viii, pp. 83—92. But that collection is also largely drawn from other, and to a great extent later, sources. [See below, pp. 56–65.]

immediate original) was ignorant of Welsh, and thus a blind
copyist and unconscious preserver of verbal forms materially
older than his own day. On the subject of this last remark,
applicable to the Genealogies still more than to the *Annales*,
and in some degree to the whole MS. of which they both
form part, more will be found in the sequel.

The *Annales* form in the MS. a part of the extensive append-
ages to one of the oldest copies of "Nennius'" *Historia
Britonum*, and the reason of their occurrence in their present
position is to be found in the desire of some copyist of the
Historia to furnish a continuation to the *Calculi*, or brief
chronological data, which are themselves added by way of
appendix to the short historical document known as the *Genealogies of the Saxon Kings*.[1] The last tract, consisting partly
of the genealogies of the various royal lines of Anglo-Saxon
England, partly of memoranda relating to early Northumbrian and early Cymric history, itself of earlier composition
than the *Historia*, was embodied with it (approximately at
the end of the ninth or beginning of the tenth century)
by intercalation between the concluding tract of the *Historia*
proper, the notice *De Arthuro et ejus prœliis*,[2] and the *Catalogue of* (British) *Cities*,[3] of which the latter had immediately
followed the former in the previous edition of the principal

[1] In the sequel we shall designate these, for brevity's sake, the
Saxon Genealogies. They were put together at various times between
the end of the seventh and middle of the eighth centuries, as is
apparent from an examination of the events and persons recorded and
mentioned therein.

[2] No edition of the *Historia* is known which does not contain this
tract ; nor are there now any means of ascertaining whether it really
formed a part of the original *Historia* (as issued in 828), or is a very
early subsequent addition.

[3] The *Catalogue of Cities* varies much in different MSS. of "Nennius".
Only a very few of the versions have yet been published. Stevenson
merely gives the one in our MS. (*Harl.* 3859). The variations are
chiefly in order and orthography.

work.[1]   And, just as the *Saxon Genealogies* were obviously
appended in the first instance in order to form a sort of
historical continuation to the note on the early history of
Bernicia which concludes the tract *De Arthuro*, and the
Annales were similarly appended to furnish a still more
marked continuation of the *Calculi*, so the Welsh Genealogies now published must have been largely intended, not
only as a "patriotic" counterpart to the previous "Saxon"
ones, but also to illustrate the two immediately preceding
historical documents by displaying the ancestry and rela-
tionships of most of the personages mentioned in both
of them.

Both *Annales* and Genealogies, *in their present form*, show
marks of having been composed in the last half of the tenth
century.   The *years* of the *Annales* are written down to
977, though the last *event* recorded is the death of Rhodri ab
Hywel Dda in 954; while the omission of the battle of
Llanrwst, which was fought in the very next year (955)
between the sons of Idwal and those of Hywel Dda (especially on the part of an annalist who, if also the composer
of the Genealogies, would seem to have been a partisan
of Hywel's family in their contest for the supremacy of
Wales), certainly points to the *Annales* having been finished
as they are now in the year 954 or 955, and never subsequently retouched.   The Genealogies commence with that

---

[1] Now represented by such MSS. as *Cott. Caligula A.* viii, or *Nero
D.* viii. It must be borne in mind that the later and amplified editions
of the *Historia* did not always completely supersede the earlier and
simpler ones ; but that in some cases the latter continued to be copied
for centuries after the former had been in existence.   Thus our MS.
(*Harl.* 3859) is older, *as a MS.*, than the two MSS. above mentioned, but
the *edition* it represents is considerably more modern than theirs.   We
may add that in some cases they preserve, not only the correcter readings, but the more archaic Welsh forms.   Mr. Stevenson's statement
(in the preface to his *Nennius*, p. xxiii), that *Calig. A.* viii contains the
Saxon Genealogies, is quite incorrect.

(given both on the father's and on the mother's side) of Owen ab Hywel Dda, who died in 988, and they must therefore have been compiled during his reign, and before that year. The frequent allusions to St. David's and its Bishops, and the almost complete absence of similar allusions to Llandaff, in the *Annales*, show these to have been composed in the former, not in the latter, see; and we are led to place the composition of the Genealogies in the same district from a consideration of the extreme meagreness and incompleteness with which they give the pedigree of the royal lines of Gwent and Morganwg, districts politically and ecclesiastically as much identified with the see of Llandaff as were Dyfed and Cardigan with that of St. David's.[1]

The date of the MS.[2] is upwards of a century later than that of the composition of the *Annales* and Welsh Genealogies which it contains; the hand (or hands ?) in which they, in common with the rest of the MS. of "Nennius" of

---

[1] Other notable omissions are those of the pedigrees of (1) Merfyn frych in the male line ; (2) of several important Cumbrian princes included in the *Bonedd Gwyr y Gogledd* in *Hengwrt MS.* 536, printed by Mr. Skene in the Appendix to his *Four Ancient Books of Wales ;* (3) of the line of Cornish princes represented by Geraint ab Erbin in about the sixth century, especially when an otherwise almost unknown line of Damnonian princes is set out in No. xxv ; (4) of the line of princes of Brycheiniog who deduced their descent from Brychan. The omission of the princes of Buallt and Gwrtheyrnion is to be accounted for by the fact that their pedigree had been already given in the preceding *Historia Britonum*. For the sake of completeness, the passage of that work containing the genealogy in question, as given in the same MS. (*Harl.* 3859), together with a few other extracts, containing early genealogies parallel to those in our text, will be printed in the next number of *Y Cymmrodor*.

[2] We are of course only speaking of the MS. of "Nennius" and "Additions to Nennius" contained in *Harl.* 3859. That MS. *volume* contains copies of many other works, which resemble the "Nennius", etc., in nothing but in being of uniform size, and written in somewhat similar hands of about the same date.

which they form part, are written, being described by the
Keeper of the MSS. in the British Museum as an English
hand of the early twelfth century. The whole MS., as it
stands, bears marks of intermediate transcription by one or
more copyists from an earlier MS. in the older " Hiberno-
Saxon" character, used in Wales up to the end of the
eleventh century.[1] The frequent and serious mistakes, both
of misspelling and wrong division, made in the transcription of the commonest or most typical Welsh names and
words, also show that at least one of the intermediate tran-
scribers cannot have been a Welshman.[2] Making allowance,

[1] This is shown by such mistakes as the following. In the *Historia*,
minmanton for *inirmanton* (the reading of *Caligula A.* viii; other
MSS. read *mirmantum* or *-tun*, or the like), fo. 178[b], l. 7, = *Stevenson*,
§ 25. In the Welsh Genealogies : *Guipno* for *Guiþno* (now *Gwyddno*),
fo. 194[a], col. 1 top : *Canantinail* for *Carantmail* (=*Carantmael*, three
times in *Red Book of Hergest*, Skene, *Four Anct. Books of Wales*,
vol. ii, p. 290), fo. 194[b], col. 3 end.   Probably the following instances
of confusion between *o*, *b*, and *d* (all in the *Saxon Genealogies*) are
also the results of copying a particular kind of " Irish" hand : (1) *Din-
guayrdi* for *Dinguayroi*, fo. 188[b], l. 4, = *S.*, § 61 end (correctly spelt
Dinguoaroy at fo. 189[a], l. 3, = *S.*, § 63); (2) *Catgublaun* for *Catguolaun*,
fo. 189[a], par. 2 (= *S.*, § 64) out of which mistake Mr. Skene has evolved
a mythic king distinct from Cadwallon ab Cadfan ; the latter is called
(with the Latin genitive termination) *Catguol. launi* (*sic*) at fo. 188[a], par.
3 (=*S.*, § 61) ; *Cat guol laun* (*sic*), fo. 190[b], col. 4 end, *Catguollaun* and
catguollaan, fo. 191[a], col. 1 top, *Catgolaum*, fo. 191[a], col. 3 top, and
Catgollaun in fo. 193[b], col. 1 top, whilst other persons of the same
name are called *Catgolaun* in fo. 193[b], col. 1, and [*C*]*atguallaun* in fo.
194[b], col. 3 top ; (3) *Eoguin* for *Edguin* (*i.e.*, King Edwin of Northumbria), fo. 189[a], ll. 5 and 6, = *S.*, § 63.
[2] Besides the mistakes enumerated in the last note, we may mention :—In the *Saxon Genealogies* : (1) *gueinth guaut* for *guenith guaut*,
fo. 188[b], ll. 9 and 10, = *S.*, § 62; (2)*Guallanc* for *Guallauc*, fo. 188[b], par. 5,
= *S.*, § 63; the name is rightly spelt in the Welsh Genealogies, fo. 194[a],
col. 1 (bottom) ; (3) *Flefaurf* for *Flefaur*, fo. 188[b] end, = *S.*, § 63 ;
rightly spelt at fo. 187[b], par. 2, = *S.*, § 57; (4) [*R*]*um* for [*R*]*un*, fo. 189[a],
par. 2, = *S.*, § 63 end (*rū* in fo. 187[b], par. 2, made by *S.*, § 57, into *Rum*;
Run in the Welsh Genealogies, fo. 193[b], col. 1, l. 9, and col. 3 *bis*, and
fo. 194[a], col. 3.). In the Welsh Genealogies: (5) *gurhaiernu* for *gurhaiernn*

however, for the nationality of the scribe (or scribes ?), it must be admitted that his general standard of literal accuracy in the transcription of so many (to him) foreign names as the MS. contains is fairly high ; and thus it is probable that the serious *lacunæ* in the sense of the short notes in Latin with which some of the Genealogies conclude (resulting in two more or less untranslatable passages), are due to transcription from defective or only partly legible originals. As has been already indicated, the non-Welsh nationality of the scribe is further shown by his preservation throughout the

(now *Gwrhaiarn*), fo. 194ᵇ, col. 3 ; (6) *Merchian*ū, for *Merchia*un (now *Meirchion*), fo. 194ᵃ, col. 1 end. The bisection and even trisection of Welsh names is noticeable everywhere ; perhaps the most extraordinary instance is at fo. 193ᵃ, col. 2 of the MS. (in the *Annales*), where the events of the year 939 are made to end with the fifth letter of the name *Clitau*c (now *Clydog*), and the next year contains the entry " uc et mouric. moritur" ! In the *Mirabilia* the scribe has copied an original *Cinlipiuc* (a district-name derived from one *Cinlip*, and in other MSS. spelt *Cinloipiauc*, from the other bye-form of the same personal name, which occurs as *Cynloyp* at fo. 194ᵃ, col. 1 of our MS.) as *Cinlipluc* (fo. 196ᵃ, par. 3 ; = *S.*, § 70), an utterly impossible form. Apparently the miscopied *i* was peculiarly formed, for the peccant *l*, though an unmistakable *l* in *form*, is only of the *height* of an *i*.

The very bad mistakes of Stevenson's edition, *Lenin* for *Lemn* of the MS., fo. 195ᵇ, par. 1, = *S.*, § 67 (the river meant is the Leven of Lennox, anciently Levenachs), and *Cataguen* for *tat aguen* of the MS. (fo. 188ᵇ, l. 8, = *S.*, § 62), the modern *tad awen*, are entirely due to the Editor, and in no way to the MS., the readings of which are perfectly clear in both instances. It is fair to say that Mr. Stevenson was generally accurate in his reproduction of this MS. (which he took for his text), though his collations of other MSS. (so far at least as relates to the forms of the proper names) cannot be implicitly relied on. In the *Saxon Genealogies*, for instance (§ 65), *manu* is given in the text as the reading of *Harl.* 3859, which reads *manau*, and the latter reading is attributed to *MS. a*, and to it alone ! Now *MS. a* is the Vatican MS., which does not contain the *Saxon Genealogies* at all ! ! The facts are that *manau* is the reading of *Harl.* 3859 alone, the other three MSS. in which the Saxon Genealogies are found (*Vespasian D.* xxi and *B.* xxv, and *Vitellius A.* xiii ; Stevenson's *MSS. B., C.* and *F.* respectively) all reading *manu*.

whole Nennian MS. of the Old-Welsh orthography,[1] which
we know from other sources to have subsisted in the latter
half of the tenth century, when (as we have seen) the
Annales and Genealogies were compiled, but to have become
obsolete by the early part of the twelfth century, when
they and the rest of the MS. were transcribed in their
present shape.[2] We may just mention here that all the
Old-Welsh forms in the MS. do not belong to the same
stage of Old-Welsh. Thus we find the form *Cuneda* in the
Historia (fo. 176[a], par. 1 ; = *Stevenson*, § 14), and six times
in the Welsh Genealogies, but the older form *Cunedag*
in the *Saxon Genealogies* (fo. 188[b], par. 4 ; = *S.*, § 62) ; on the
other hand, the river Teifi is called by its older form *Tebi* at
the end of the Welsh Genealogies (fo. 195[a], col. 3, par. 2), but
Teibi in the *Historia* (fo. 185[a], l. 9 ; = *S.*, § 47) ; whilst in

[1] The only exceptions that we have been able to find to this rule
are : (*a*) The name *Ceneu*, which (assuming it to stand for the
modern name *Cenau* found in *Llangenau*, which it has always been
considered to do) should certainly in Old-Welsh be *Cenou*, and *Ceneu*
only in Middle-Welsh. *Ceneu* occurs thrice (twice with the *u* accented)
on fo. 194[a] of the MS. *Cenew* (for which the Old-Welsh would be
Ceneu) does not seem to be an authenticated Welsh name. (*b*) The
name *Catleu*, in fo. 194[a], col. 3 ; but this may be the Old-Welsh form
of a name *Cadlew*, just as well as the Middle-Welsh one of a name
Cadlau. It should be borne in mind that Middle-Welsh peculiarities
do occur, though very rarely, in the oldest Welsh Glosses, and that
the Old-Welsh pronunciation had probably been given up for some
time before the orthography representing it became obsolete.

[2] The *Liber Landavensis*, of which the original MS., completed in
about 1133, and therefore nearly contemporary with the " Nennius",
etc., of *Harl.* 3859, still exists, presents very numerous specimens of
Welsh, in many of which the chief Middle-Welsh peculiarities are so
constantly intruding as to show that the latter must then have been
well established. The fact that the language of these specimens is
to a very great extent Old-Welsh must be attributed to the circum-
stance that they chiefly consist of the boundaries and attestations
contained in copies of old grants of land to the Bishops of Llandaff ;
and of such documents it was naturally considered highly important
to put on record, as far as possible, the exact original forms.

the *Annales*, the district of Brycheiniog is called by its older
form *Broceniauc* under the year 848 (fo. 192^b, col. 1, top),
but *Bricheniauc* under the year 895 (fo. 192^b, col. 3, middle).

The historical value of the *Annales* is so well known and
so universally recognised, that we have considered it superfluous to dilate upon it here. Our own investigations into
such of the Welsh Genealogies as admit of being checked by
comparison with collateral authorities (such as the *Annales*,
the various Irish Annals, and the scattered indications of
the facts of early Welsh history to be gleaned from other
authentic sources) is, that up to the date when all Welsh
records necessarily become more or less fabulous, these Genealogies have every claim to rank beside the *Annales* and
the *Saxon Genealogies* as a valuable historical authority.
Allowance must of course be made for such mistakes as are
naturally incident to the transcription of pedigrees written
in narrow columns of a name to a line; the most important of which are (1) the frequent omission of names,
and (2) the occasional repetition of the word *map*, " son",
where it ought not to be repeated, by which means a man's
epithet is wrongly made to appear as though it were the
name of his father, whilst his real father is put back one
generation. But a little knowledge of Welsh personal names,
and occasional reference to later versions of the pedigrees,
will enable anyone readily to correct most of these blunders.
As to the philological value of both *Annales* and Genealogies, it will be enough to point out that they contain several
hundred Welsh words (chiefly names of persons and places),
in their Old-Welsh forms. No other such repertory of Old-
Welsh proper names exists; the older collection of them in
the *Book of St. Chad* being very scanty, and the later ones in
the *Liber Landavensis* and in the Lives of the Welsh Saints
(chiefly contained in *Cott. Vesp. A.* xiv) being largely inter-
mixed with Middle-Welsh forms.

We have considered the importance of our whole text to
warrant our reproducing it line for line, exactly as in the
MS., where it is written continuously in columns of three
or four to the page. A fair specimen of the handwriting
and style of the MS. will be found in the facsimile of
fo. 192ᵃ, prefixed to the printed *Annales Cambriæ*. In the
MS. the columnar arrangement is continued to the end of
the *Catalogue of Cities*, which we have therefore included
here ; and we have also, in order to show the position of
the *Annales* relatively to the other " Additions" to the
Historia Britonum, reprinted the *Calculi*, which the annalist
clearly intended to serve as a ready-made preface to his
appended chronicle. Both the *Catalogue* and the *Calculi*
will be found in Stevenson's edition of " Nennius", where
the second forms § 66, and the first is printed by way of
appendix on p. 62.

Two letter-forms occur in the MS. which, in consequence
of the lack of proper type, we have not been able exactly to
reproduce. The first of these is the second or short form of *r*,
which in our MS., when in the middle of a word, is sometimes
almost indistinguishable from *i*. This we have represented by
the character " ɪ". The second is the well-known mediæval
character for the diphthong *æ* (in our MS. an *e* with a loop
underneath it), which we have rendered by simply *italicising*
the ordinary diphthong. In the case of a *capital* letter, the
MS. almost always writes the diphthong in full. With regard
to the letter *i*, the practice of the MS. is irregular. Sometimes it marks the *i*'s with the common acute stroke over
them, sometimes not. Wherever the stroke occurs, we have
reproduced it ; where it is omitted, we have dotted the letter.
We may add here that an identical stroke or accent sometimes occurs over other vowels, and in every case has been
reproduced. Two kinds of *d* occur in the MS., one with an
upright, the other with a bent-back, upward stroke. The latter

is by far the rarer, and is represented by the character "ð". As a rule the letter *v* only occurs in the MS. as a capital or a substitution for a cancelled letter, the short *s* only as a capital or at the end of lines, or in substitution. We only give hyphens where they are given in the MS. Contractions (the Latin ones are often arbitrary, or at least unusual, and throughout there is no distinction between the contractions for *m* and *n*) are extended in italics,[1] and the initial capitals of each genealogy, etc., omitted through the neglect of the rubricator to supply them, are supplied by us (as far as possible) in black-letter type within square brackets. The Genealogies have been consecutively numbered in Roman figures, to facilitate future reference, and the dates of the events, taken from the published editions, have been similarly supplied in the *Annales*.[2]

[1] With the exception of (1) the contraction for "An*nus*", heading every year in the *Annales*, which we have left as in the MS.; (2) sometimes the contractions for " Iesus Christus" (*ih's xpc* or the like), and for " Dominus noster" (*dn's n'r*), and (3) one of the contractions for *et*, very similar to the modern *&*, by which we have represented it.

[2] It was the intention of the writer to have accompanied both the fourteenth-century Genealogies from *Jesus College* (Oxon.) *MS.* 20 (printed in *Y Cymmrodor*, vol. viii, pp. 83—92) and the ones now printed with translations and extensive critical notes, the latter embracing a comparison of the corresponding genealogies in the two MSS. with each other and with the other early authorities. The state of his health prevented his carrying out this plan; but he hopes to be able to perform the very necessary task in a slightly different form some time during the coming year. All he is able to do at present is to give an exact text of the Harleian Genealogies, with a few critical notes, merely relating to the readings of the MS.

[For the Jesus College Genealogies, see below, pp. 56-65.]

[*Fo. 189ᵇ, middle.]

[TEXT.]

A. D.
[457.] *[**A**] mundi principio uſq*ue* ad conſtantinu*m* & rufu*m* .
quinq*ue* milia ſexcenti quinquaginta octo anni rep*er*iuntu*r* .

[29. 400.] Item aduobuſ geminiſ rufo & rubelio uſq*ue* in ſtillitionem¹
conſule*m* . c̈c̈c̈ . ſeptuaginta treſ anniſ .   Item a ſtillitione¹

[425. uſq*ue* adualentinianu*m* filiu*m* placide & regnu*m* guorthigirni .
uiginti octo anni .   Et aregno² guorthigirni . uſq*ue* ad diſ-

[436.] cordia*m* guitolini & ambroſíí . anni ſunt duodeci*m* . quodeſt
guoloppvm³. ideſt catguoloph .   Guorthigirnuſ aute*m* tenuit

[425.] imp*er*ium inbrittannia theo doſio & ualentiniano conſulibuſ .

[428.] & in quarto anno regni ſui ſaxoneſ adbrittanniam⁴. uener*unt* .
Felice & tauro conſulibuſ . quadringenteſimo anno . ab incar-
natione d*o*m*i*ni n*oſt*ri ih'u xp'i .

[**A**]b anno quo ſaxoneſ uener*unt* inbrittannia*m* . & aguor-
[? 497 thigirno⁵ ſuſcep- [fo. 190ᵃ]ti ſunt ⸴ uſq*ue* ad deciu*m* &
or 498.] ualerianu*m* . anni ſunt ſexaginta nouem .

[445.] *an'	[*col. 1.]	an'	
an'		an'	
an'		an'	
an'		an'	
an'		an'. Paſca com	[453]
		mvtatur⁶ ſup*er* di-	

---

¹ Read *Stillicionem* (*i.e.* "Stilichonem") and -*e* respectively.

² There is a "caret" between the *e* and the *g* of this word, but
no letter inserted overline. Probably the alteration contemplated
was into *rengno*. The mark cannot be read (as a contraction) with the
line below.

³ The *v* of this word written in substitution over an expuncted *o* ;
and its *m* altered from an *n*. These and all other alterations or
additions mentioned in these notes are made by the scribe of the MS.,
unless specified to be otherwise.

⁴ The *d* of this word is added overline.

⁵ The *a* of this word is similarly added.

⁶ The *v* of this word written in substitution over an expuncted *o*.

A.D.			A.D.
	em *dominicum* cum[1]	an'	
	papa leone . epiſcopo	an'	
	rome .	an'	
[454.]	an' . x . Brigida[2]	an'	
	ſancta naſcitur .	an'	
	an'	an'	
	an'	an'	
[457.]	an' *Sanctuſ* Patriciuſ	an'	
	ad *dominum* migra-	an' . xl .	
	tur .	an'	
	an'	an'	
	an'	an'	
	an'	an'	
	an'	an'	
	an'	an' .	
	an'	an'	
	an' . xx .	an' .	
	an'	an . l .[4]	
	an'	an'	
	an'	an'	
[468.]	an' quieſ benigni	an'	
	epiſcopi[3] .	an'	
	an'	an'	
	an'	an'	
	an'	an' Epiſcopuſ ebur pau- [501]	
	an'.	fat in*chri*ſto an	
	an'	no . cccl . etatiſ	
	an' . xxx . [*col. 2.]	ſuæ[5]	
	an'	an'	

---

[1] Apparently mis-translated from Old-Welsh *cant*, " by *or* with," now *gàn.*   [2] The *d* of this word altered from a *t.*

[3] An ſ originally written after *ep'i* and then partly erased.

[4] One year too few between years *xl* and *l*; the blunder rectified afterwards by the insertion of one year too many between years *lx* and *lxx.*

[5] See O'Donovan's *Annals of the Four Masters*, vol. i, p. 163.

A.D.   A.D.

an'   an'
an' . lx .   an'
an'   an'
an'   an'
an'   an'
an'   an'
*an'   [*col. 3.]   an'
an'   an'
an'   an'
an'   an' . xc .
an'   an'
an'   an'
an' . lxx .   an'   Gueith cam lann² inqua [537.]
an' .   arthur & medraut
[516.] an' Bellum badonif inquo   corruerunt . et mortali-
       arthur portauit crucem   [taf
       domini nostri ihu xp'i . tribuſ   *inbrit-   [*fo. 190ᵇ, col. 1.]
       diebuſ & tribuſ noctibuſ   tannia
       inhumerof fuof &   et in hiber
       brittonef uictozef fuerunt .   nia fuit .³
       an'
       an'   an'
       an'   an'
       an'   an'
[521.] an' Sanctuf columcille naf-   an'
                            [citur .   an'
           Qui eſ¹ fanctœ brigidœ .   an'
       an'   an' . c . dormitatio   [544.]
       an'   ciarani .
       an' . lxxx .   an'

---

¹ Read *Quieſ*.

² The second *n* of this word added overline.

³ Part of this and all the preceding three lines written over an
erasure. There are some remains of the erased letters.

A.D.

an'

[547.] an' . Mor-

talitaſ

magna

inqua

pauſat

mailcun

rex gene

dotæ[1] .

·an'

an'

an'

an'

an'

an'

an' . cx .

an'

an'

an'

◂[558] an' Gabr-

an . filiuſ

dungart :

moritur .

an'

an'

an'

[562.] an' Colum-

*cillæ inbrit-　　　　　　[*col. 2.]

tannia ex-

ſít .

an'

A.D.

an' exx .

an'

an'

an'

an'

an'

an' . Gildaſ　　　　　　[570.]

obíít .

an'

an'

an' Bellum　　　　　　[573.]

armterid .[2]

an' cxxx ⸗　　　　　　[574.]

Brendan

býror doʐ

mitatio .

an'

an' .

an'

an'

an'

an' Guur-　　　　　　[580.]

ci et peretur

moritur .

an'

an',

an'

an' . cxl .　　　　　　[584.]

Bellum con-

tra eubo-

niam et diſ-

---

1 Read *guenedotæ*.
2 *An'* erased just before *armterid* in the same line.

A.D.

poſitio¹ da-
nieliſ ban-
corum .
an' .
*an'   [*col. 3.]
an'
an'
[589.] an' . Conuerſio *con*
       ſtantini ad
       *do*minu*m* .
an'
an'
an'
an'
an' . cl .
[595.] an'   Colu*m*cille mo
       ritu*r* . Dunaut
       rex moritu*r*² .

Aguſtinuſ mellituſ
angloſ ad *chriſtu*m
*co*nuertit .
an'
an'
an'
an'
an'

an' . Sinoduſ urbiſ   [601.]
legion . Gre-
goriuſ obíít in
*chriſt*o . Dauid³
epiſcopuſ moni iu-
deoru*m* .
an'
an'
an' . clx .
an
an' . Diſpoſitio¹   [606.]
cinauc epiſcopi .
an'   Aidān⁴ map   [607.]
gabran moritu*r* .
an'
an'
an'
*an'   [*col. 4.]
an'
an' . Conthigirni   [612.]
obitu*ſ* et dibric epiſcopi .
an' . Gueith cair   [613.]
legion . *et* ibi ceci-
dit ſeli*m* filíí⁵ cinan .
Et iacob filíí be-
li dor*mitatio* .⁶
an' . clxx .⁷
an'

---

¹ Read *depoſitio*.   ² Inadequately altered from in*oritur*.
³ *Et* is apparently omitted before *Dauid*.
⁴ The scribe originally meant, probably, to write " Aidan", and afterwards wrote the *n* in full ; but the mark of contraction is not the usual one. In the interval between this line and the next, just between the *d* of *Aidan* and the *b* of *Gabran*, some letter has been erased.
⁵ Read *filiuſ*.   ⁶ Or " dor*mitat*"?
⁷ One year too many between *clx* and *clxx*.

A.D.
[616.] an' Ceretic obíit .

[617.] an' . Et guin[1] in-
cip*it* regnare .

an'

an'

an'

an'

an'

an . clxxx .

[624.] fol obfcurat*uſ eſt*

an' .

[626.] an' . Etguin
baptizat*uſ eſt ꞉*
Et run fili*uſ* urb-
gen baptiza-
uit eu*m*.

[627.] an . Belin mo*2*it*ur* .

A.D.

an' .

an' . obfeffio cat   [629.]
guol laun[2] re-
gif ininfula
glannauc .

an' . Guidgar   [630.]
uenit *et* n*on*
redit . k*a*lend*iſ*[3] . ia-
nuar*iiſ*[4] . gueith[5] meicen *et* ibi inter-
*fect*uſ eſt* et guiñ .[6]   [*fo. 191ᵃ, col. 1.]
cu*m* duob*uſ* filííſ
fuiſ . Catguo
llaun[7] aute*m*
uictor fuit .

an' . Bellu*m* cant   [631.]
fcaul[8] inquo cat-
guollaan[9] corruit .

---

¹ Read *Etguin*.

³ The *k* of this contraction is of a very unusual form.

⁴ The second *a* of this word is added above the line. The *caret* under-neath, indicating where the letter is to come in, happens to stand just above the second *e* of *Meicen* in the line below, and being indistinguishable in form from the contraction used in this MS. for *er*, was carelessly copied as such, though it had already done duty for *ianuariſ* in the line above. Hence the gibberish *Meiceren* of the printed editions. The battle is mentioned as *Bellum Meicen* in the *Saxon Genealogies, supra*, fo. 188ᵃ, par. 3 (= *S.*, § 61). *MS. B.* has *Bellum Meigen* here ; and the place is frequently mentioned as *Meigen* in Middle-Welsh (*e.g.*, in the *Red Book of Hergest*, cols. 592 and 1043). It is odd that Mr. Skene, who, in his *Chronicles of the Picts*, etc. (1867), p. 14, correctly reads *Meicen* here, should quote the passage as reading *Meiceren* in his *Four Ancient Books*, etc. (1868), vol. i, p. 70.

⁵ The *e* of this word added above the line.

⁶ Read *Etguin ;* the word was first written " et guu*2*", and the last two letters subsequently altered so as to make " -in".

⁷ Originally written with a full stop after the *ll*, afterwards utilised towards making the first *a*.

⁸ The *l* of this word (spelt *Catscaul* in the *Saxon Genealogies, supra*, fo. 189ᵃ, par. 2 = *S.*, § 64), is added overline.   ⁹ Read *catguollaun*.

A.D.
[632.] an' . Stragef fabri-
ne & iugulatio
iudrif .
an' .
an' . cxc .
an' .
an' .
an' .
an' .
an' .
an' .
an' .
an' .
an' .
[644.] an' . cc . Bellum coc
boý[1] inquo ofuuald .
rex nordorum &eo-
ba rex merciorum
corruerunt .
[645.] an' . Percufio[2] de
meticæ regionif .
quando cenobi-
um dauid incenfum eſt .
an' .

an' .
an' .
an' .
an' . Ortuſ ftellæ .   [650.]
an' .
an' .
an' .
*an' cc . x .   [*col. 2.]
an'
an' . Stragef gaíí   [656.]
campi .
an' . Pantha occifio .   [657.]
an' . Ofguid[3] uenit .   [658.]
et predam duxit .
an' .
an' .
an' . Commene   [661.]
fota[4] .
an' . broc mail[5] . mo   [662.]
ritur .
an'
an' . cc . xx .
an' . Primum pafca   [665.]
apud faxonef cele-

---

[1] Altered from cocboï. The name is spelt Cocboy, supra, fo. 189[b], par. 2 (= S., § 65, p. 55), and might now be either Cochfy, Cochfwy, Cogfy, or Cogfwy ; the corresponding passage in the later Chronicle (MS. B of the printed edition) has Chochui.

[2] First written percutio; the t is expuncted, and the ſ written above it.

[3] There is a letter erased after this word ; ? an i, so as to have originally made Osguidi ? The t of Pantha seems altered from a c.

[4] "Cummine the tall (dies)."

[5] Read brocmail. Brochwel Ysgythrog, whose grandson Selyf was killed in 613 (see above), cannot possibly be meant, if the date 662 is right.

A.D.

bratur . Bellum bado-
nif fecundo[1] . morcant
moritur .
an' .
an'
an'
[669.] an' Ofguid rex
faxonum moritur .
an' .
an' .
an' .
an' .
an' .[2]
an' . ccxxx .
an' .
[676.] an' . Stella mi-
re inagnitudi-
nif[3] . uifa *eft* per totum mundum lu-
cenf .
an' .
an' .
*an' .   [*col. 3.]

A.D.

an' .
an' .
an' . Mortalitaf magna   [682.]
fuit in brittannia . n qua[4]
catgualart filiuf catguo-
l-aum[5] obíít .
an' . Mortalitaf inhiber-   [683.]
nia .
an' . ccxl . Terre motuf   [684.]
in eubonia[6] factuf eft magnuf.
an' .
an' .
an' .
an' .
an' . Pluuia fanguinea   [689.]
facta eft in brittannia .
et lac . *et* butirum uerfa
íunt in fanquinem[7] .
an' .
an' .
an' .
an' .
an' . ccl .

---

[1] This is apparently the battle called *Bedan-* or *Biedan-heafod* in the *Saxon Chronicle*, and there placed under the year 675. Mistakes of ten years were readily made through the omission or addition of a single *x* by an inadvertent copyist. The similarity between the English name and that of Mount Badon (see the year 516, to which the reference is) was probably but accidental.

[2] *Annus* occurs once too often in this decade. The second *c* of *ccxxx* is added above the line.   [3] Read *magnitudinif.*

[4] Read *inqua.*   [5] *Sic* MS. Read *Catguolaun* or -ni.

[6] There is an erasure (apparently of a stop) after this word.

[7] Exactly the same sentence in the version of the Saxon Chronicle contained in *Cott. Domitian A* . viii, " Here wearþ on Brytene blodi ren. ꝺ meolc ꝺ butere wurdon gewend to blode", but under the year 685.

A.D.

A.D.

an'.

an'.

an'.

an'. Oſbrit rex ſaxo- [717.]
num moritur.

an'..

an'. Confecracio mi- [718.]
chaeliſ archange-
li æcclefiæ.

an'.

an'.

an'.

an'.

an'.

an'.

an'. Æſtaſ torrida. [721.]

an'.¹

an'. Beli filiuſ elfin mo- [722.]
ritur. & bellum hehil
apud cornuenſeſ. gue-
ith gart mailauc.
Cat pencon. apud
dexteraleſ britto
neſ. & brittoneſ
uictoreſ fueunt. in
iſtiſ tribuſ belliſ.

[704.] an'. cclx. Alch frit² rex
ſaxonum obíit.
Dormitatio adomnan.

an'.

an'.

*an'. [*fo. 191ᵇ, col. 1.]

an'.

an'.

an'.

an'. cclxxx.

an'.

an'.

an'.

an'.

an'.

an'.

an'.

[714.] an'. cc.lxx. Nox lu-
cida³ fuit ficut
dieſ. pipínuſ maioꝛ
rex francorum obí-
it in chriſto.

an'. Bellum mortiſ⁴ [728.]
carno.

an'.

*an'. [*col. 2.]

an'.

an'.

¹ *Annus* is inserted once too often in this decade.
² Read *Alchfrit*.
³ *An'* erased at the beginning of this line.
⁴ Read *montiſ*. The place, called *Monitcarno* in the *Annals of Ulster*, s. a. 729, was in Central Scotland ("juxta Stagnum Loogdae", i.e., apparently Loch Tay), not in Wales.

A.D.

an' .

an' .

an' .[1]

an' . ccxc .

[735.] an' . Beda preſbiter
dormit .

[736.] an' . Ougen rex pic-
torum obíít .

an' .

an' .

an' .

an' .

an' .

an' .

an' .

an' . ccc .

an' .

an' .

an' .

an' .

an' .

[750.] an' . Bellum inter pic-
toſ & britto-
neſ . id eſt gueiht[2].
moce tauc[3] .

Et rex eorum
talargan . a
brittonibuſ oc-
ciditur . teudubr[4]
filiuſ beli moritur .

an' .

an' .

an' .

an' . cccx . Rotri   [754.]
rex brittonum .
moritur .

an' .

an' .[5]

an' . Eðpalð rex ſaxo   [757.]
num moritur[5].

*an' .   [*col. 3.]

an' .

an' . Bellum inter   [760.]
brittoneſ et ſaxo-
neſ . id eſt gueith .
hirford . & dun-
nagual filíí teu-
dubr[6] . moritur .

an' .

an' .

---

1 *An'* is inserted once too often in this decade.

2 The *h* of this word is added above the line. The word should
be *gueith* in the usual orthography.

3 Read *mocetauc*.

4 The *b* of this word is added above the line.

5 These two years and the events of the second are added in the
same hand after the end of the original column ; and the first year of
the next column is similarly prefixed to the original column.

6 Read *dumnagual filiuf teudubr*. The *b* of the last word is added
above the line.

A.D.

an'.

an'. cccxx.

an'.

an'.

an'.

[768.] an'. Paſca com-
mutat*ur* ap*ud* britt-
toneſ em*en*dante
elbodugo homi-
ne dei.

an'.

an'.

an'.

an'.

an'.

[775.] an'. ccc.xxx.

an'. Fernmail
fili*uſ* iudhail mo-
rit*ur*.

[776.] an'. Cenioẏd[1]
rex pictoru*m* obiit.

[777.] an'. Cudberth[2] abba*ſ*
morit*ur*.

[778.] an'. Vaſtatio britt-
tonum dexterali-
u*m* ap*ud*[3] offa.

A.D.

an'.

an'.

an'.

an'.

*an'.   [*fo. 192ᵃ, col. 1.]

an'. cccxl. Vaſta-   [784.]
ti[4] brittonu*m*. cu*m*[5] of-
fa ineſtate.

an'.

an'.

an'.

an'.

an'.

an'.

an'.

an'.

an'.[6]

an'. ccc.l.

an'. Prim*uſ* aduen-   [796.]
tuſ gentiliu*m*. ap*ud*
dexteraleſ adhi-
berniam.

an'. Offa rex mer-   [796.]
cioru*m*. & morge-
tiud[7]. rex deme-

---

[1] Altered from *Cenioid*.

[2] The *h* of this word added above the line.

[3] Probably a mistake in copying *ap* = *ab*. "By Offa", and not "in Offa's country", is apparently meant.

[4] We must either read *Vaſtatio* or *brittoneſ*.

[5] This must be a mistake in translating the Old-Welsh *cant* (now *gàn*), which meant "by" as well as "with".

[6] *An'* repeated once too often in this decade.

[7] The *o* of this word was begun as an *e*. See the "facsimile" of the page in *Annales Cambriæ*.

A.D.

torum . morte mo-
riuntur . et bellum
rud glann .
an' .

[798.] an' . Caratauc rex
guenedote apud
faxonef iugulatur .
an' .
an' .
an' .
an' .
an' .
an' . ccc . lx .
an' .
an' .

[807.] an' . Arthgen[1] rex
cereticiaun
*moritur .   [*col. 2.]

[808.] an' . regin rex demeto-
rum . & catell[2] pouif moriuntur .

[809.] an' . Elbodg[3] archi epifcopuf
guenedote[4] . regione

A.D.

migrauit ad domi-
num .
An' . Combuftio mi-   [810.]
niu .
an' . Eugem[5] filiuf mar-   [811.]
getiud moritur .
an' . De cantorum[6] ictu   [812.]
fulminif comburit[7] .
an' . Bellum inter hi-   [813.]
guel[8] uictoʒ fuit .
an' .[9]
an' . ccc . lxx .   [814.]
Tonitruum mag-
num fuit et incendia
multa fecit .
Trifun filiuf regin
moritur .
Et grip hiud[10] fi-
liuf cincen dolofa
difpenfatione a
fratre fuo elized
poft inter uallum duo-
rum menfium inter-

---

1 The *th* of this word added above the line.
2 The second *l* of this word similarly added.
3 The *d* of this word similarly added. Read *Elbodug*, or *Elbodg*u.
4 *In* should apparently precede this word.
5 Read *Euge*in.
6 Read *Decantorum* arx.
7 The contraction for *-ur*, making *combur*itur, has perhaps been omitted to be copied by the scribe.
8 The words *et Kinan, Higuel* are omitted here, as is shown by the reading of *MS. B.*
9 *Annuf* repeated once too often in this decade.
10 Read *griphiud*. '

A.D.

ficit*ur* . Higuel
demonia infv-
la¹ triumpha-
uit . *et* cinan de
ea expulit . cu*m*
contritione mag-
na exercit*uſ* fui .
an’
[816.] an’ . Higuel it*erum*
*demonia expulſ*uſ*eſt* [*col. 3.]
Cinan rex morit*ur* .
[817.] an’ . Gueith lannmaéſ² .
an’ .
an’ .
an’ .
an’ .
[822.] an’ . Arc*em* detantor*um*³
aſaxonib*uſ* deſtruit*ur* .
et region*em* poẏuiſ
in sua poteſtate
traxer*unt* .
an’ .
an’ . ccclxxx .

A.D.

an’ Higuel morit*ur* .   [825.]
an’ .
an’ .
an’ .
an’ .
an’ .
an’ . Laudent morit*ur* .   [831.]
    et ſat*ur*biu⁴ hail
    miniu morit*ur* .
an’
an’
an’ . ccc . xc .
an’
an’
an’
an’
an’
an’ . Nobiſ ep*iſcopuſ*   [840.]
    inminiu reg-
    nauit . An’⁵. An’⁵. Iud   [842.]
      [guoll[au*n*]
      morit[*ur* .]
an’

---

¹ The *v* of this word is written above the line in substitution for an expuncted *o*.

² The second *n* of this word added above the line ; and the accent over the *e* appears to be a subsequent addition, but probably an old accent has been merely inked over, as is occasionally done in this MS. with the strokes over the *i*'s, when the old strokes are sometimes still discernible underneath the new ones.

³ Read *decantorum*.   ⁴ ? "ſat*ur* biu", MS. Read *ſaturnbiu*.

⁵ These two years and the events of the second were added thus by the scribe, after the completion of the column where they should have found a place. The last parts of the two last words, which extended to the right margin of the page, have been cut off by the binder. That the name, when perfect, was (that now spelt) *Idwallon*, and not

A.D.

[844.] an' . cccc . mermin
moritur . gueith
cetill[1].
*an'.   [*fo. 192[b], col. 1.]
an' .
an' .
[848.] an' . gueit finnant
iuðhail[2] . rex gue-
nt . auirif broce-
niauc . occifuf *eft*
[849.] an' . Mouric occi*fuf eft*
afaxonib*uf* .
[850.] an' . Cinnen agen-
tilib*uf* iugulat*ur* .
an' .
an' .
[853.] an' . Mon uaftata
agentilib*uf* nig*rif* .
[854] an' . cccc . x . Cinnen
rex pouif . inro-
ma obíit .
an'
[856] an'. Cemoẏth[3] rex

pictor*um* mo*r*itur .
& ionathan
princepf op*er*-
gelei mo*r*itur .
an' .
an' .
an' .
an' .
an' .
an' . Cat gueithen[4] .   [862.]
expulf*uf eft*
an'
an' . cccc . xx . du-   [864.]
ta uaftauit
gliuifigng[5] .
an' . Ciannant in   [865]
mer[6] obíit .
an' . Vrbf ebrauc .   [866.]
uaftata eft id *eft* cat   [*col. 2.]
dub gint[7].
an' .
an' .
an' . Cat brin onnen[8] .   [869.]

Idwal, is not only indicated by the orthography of what remains, but proved by the fact that MS. B here reads *Idwalaum* for *Idwal(l)aun*, the Middle-Welsh for our *Iudguollaun*.

1 The *t* of this word altered from a prior *c*.
2 Altered from *iuthail*.
3 Similarly altered from *Cemoith*. Read *Cenioyth*.
4 Read *Catgueithen*.
5 A mistake, apparently, for *gliguifing*.
6 MS. B, which reads *Chian nant newer*, enables us to restore the right reading, *Cian nant nimer* "Cian of Nant Nyfer" (now *Nanhyfer* or Nevern in Cemmes, N. Pembrokeshire) here.
7 ="York City was wasted ; *i.e.*, the Battle with the Black Heathen (the Danes)."   8 ="The Battle of Ashdown."

A.D.
[870.] an' . Arx alt clut .
　　　　agentilibu∫ frac-
　　　　ta e∫t

[871.] an' . Guoccaun
　　　　mer∫u∫ e∫t rex ce-
　　　　tericiaun[1] .

　　　an'

[873.] an' . Nobi∫ et mou-
　　　　ric moriuntur .
　　　　gueith bannguo-
　　　　lou[2] .

　　　an' . cccc . xxx .

[875.] an' . Dungarth[3] rex
　　　　cerniu . mer∫u∫e∫t .

[876.] an' . gueith[4] diu ∫ul
　　　　inmón .

[877.] an' . Rotri et filiu∫
　　　　eiu∫ guriat a∫a-
　　　　xonibu∫ iugu-
　　　　latur .

[878.] an' . Aed map neill
　　　　moritur .

　　　an' .

an' . Gueit conguoẏ　　　　A.D.
　　　digal rotri a-　　　　[880.]
　　　deo[5] .

an' .

an' . Cat gueithen[6] .　　　[882.]
　　　obiit .

an' .

an' . cccc . xl .

an' . Higuel inro-　　　　　[885.]
　　　ma de funtu∫ e∫t

*an' .　　　　　　　[*col. 3.]

an' . Cerb all[7] de-　　　　[887.]
　　　functu∫ e∫t

an' .

an' .

an' .

an' .

an' . Himeẏd　　　　　　[892.]
　　　moritur[8] .

an' .

an' . cccc . l . Ana-　　　　[894.]
　　　raut cum an-
　　　gli∫ uenit ua∫-

---

[1] Read *cereticiaun.*

[2] The second *n* of this word added above the line.

[3] Or "Dumgarth"? We should expect "Dumngarth", especially as *MS. B* reads *Dumnarth.* But cf. *Dungart, supra,* under the year 558, and the Old-Cornish form *Donierth* on the stone at St. Clere's.

[4] The *h* of this word is partly written over a smudge. Probably *gueit* was the word as originally written. The Welsh words mean "Sunday's Battle in Anglesey".

[5] = "The Battle of the Conway; a vengeance for Rhodri at the hand of God."

[6] Read *Catgueithen.*

[7] Read *Cerball.*

[8] *An'* (wrongly) written and then erased, before this word.

A.D.

tare ceretici-
aun . *et* ſtrat
tui[1] .

[895.] an' . Hord mani[2]
uener*unt* . *et* uaſ-
tauer*unt* loẏcr .
et bricheniauc
et guent . *et* guinn
liguiauc .

an' .

an' .

an' .

an' .

[900.] an' . Albrit rex
giuoẏſ[3] . mo*i*i-
t*ur* .

an' .

[902.] an' . Igmunt in-
inſula món

A.D.

uenit . *et* tenu-
it maeſ oſme-
liavn[4] .

an' . Loumarch   [903.]
filiuſ hiemid[5] .
moritur .

*an' . cccc . lx .   [*fo. 193ª, [904.]
                        col. 1.]
Roſtri[6] de cole[7] *eſt*
in arguiſtli .

an' .

an' . Gueith dinme-   [906.]
ir . *et* miniu[8] fra-
cta*eſt*

an' . Guorchiguil   [907.]
morit*ur* .

an' . aſſer defunct*uſ eſt* .   [908.]

an' . Catell[9] rex mo-   [909.]
rit*ur*[10] .

an' .

---

[1] Read *tiui*. *Ystrad Tywi* is meant.   [2] Read *Nordmani*.

[3] = "King of the Gewissi", *i.e.*, of Wessex.

[4] The *v* of this word added above the line.

[5] Altered from a prior *hiemit* by the scribe. The name should have been written *himeit* or *himeid* (now *Hyfaidd*).

[6] This is for *Rotri* (now *Rhodri*); but perhaps the form *Rostri* (which is believed to occur elsewhere) is not a mistake, but analogous to such Anglo-Saxon forms as *Bristric* for *Brihtric*, etc., mentioned in *The Academy* for Jan. 28, 1888 (No. 821, New Series, p. 59, col. 1). *Cair Carastauc*, for *C. Caratauc*, is said to occur in the Vatican MS. of the *Historia Britonum*, apud *Monumenta Historica Britannica*, Preface, p. 68, note 5, col. 1.

[7] This must be a mistake for *decoll'* (i.e., *decollatus*, the reading of MS. B.)

[8] A letter has been erased immediately after the end of this word.

[9] The second *l* of this word is a subsequent addition of the scribe's in a different ink, and the last part of it is written over an erased letter or stop.   [10] *An'* written before *-ritur*, and then erased.

A.D.
an' .
an' .
[913.] an' . Otter uenit .
an' . cccc.lxx .
[915.] an' . Anaraut rex
moritur .
an' .
[917.] an' . Ælfled regi-
na obíít .
an' .
[919.] an' Clitauc rex
occifuſeſt .
an' .
[921.] an' Gueith dinas¹
neguid .
an' .
an' .
an' . cccc . lxxx .
an' .
an' .
an' .
[928.] an' . Higuel rex
perrexit adro-
mam .
an' .
an' .

*an' .   [*col. 2.]   A.D.
an' .
an' .
an' . cccc . xc .
an' .
an' .
an' .
an' . Bellum brune .   [938.]
an' . Himeid filiuſ   [939.]
clita .
an'² . uc et mouric .
moritur .
an' . Ædelſtan mo-   [941.]
ritur .
an' .
an' . Abloÿc rex mo-   [942.]
ritur .
an' . Catel filiuſ art-   [943.]
mail . ueneno
moritur . et iud-
gual . et filiuſ eiuſ
elized . a faxo-
nibuſ occiduntur .
an' . ꝺ . Lunberth³ .   [944.]
epiſcopuſ inminiu
obíít .

¹ The short *s* of this word is written over the line to save space. Within the line, a long *ſ* would have been used.

² Of course we must re-unite *clita-uc* (the name now written *Clydog*) and cancel this *an(nuſ)*, which (to say nothing of its absurd position, bisective of a proper name) makes a year too many in the decade.

³ "Lumberth" might equally well be read. *Lūbert.* was first written by the scribe, then something now erased (? the beginning of *ep'ſ;* it extends both above and below the line). The *h* was then squeezed in a little above the line between the *t* and the erasure, after the latter had been made.

A.D.

A.D.

an' .

an'

[946.] an' . Cincenn[1] filiuſ elized ueneno períít .
 et eneuriſ epiſcopuſ[2]
 miniú obíít .
 Et ſtrat clut .
 uaſtataeſt aſaxo-
 nibuſ .

[947.] an' . Eadmund[3] rex
 ſaxonum iugu-
  latur[4] eſt

an' .

an' .

[950.] an' . Higuel rex
 *brittonum obíít . [*col. 3.]

[? 951.] an' . Et cat guocaun[5]
 filiuſ ouein . a[6] ſaxo-
 nibuſ iugulatur . Et
 bellum carno .

an' .

an' .

[954.] an' . ꝺx . Rotri filiuſ
 higuel moʑitur .

an' .

an' .

an' .

an' .

an' .

---

an'

an' .

an'

an'

an' . ꝺxx .

an'

an'

an'

an'

an'

an'

an' .

an' .

an' .

an' . ꝺxxx .

an' .

an'

an' .   [977.]

[I.]

[Ꝺ]uen map iguel .
 map . catell[7] .
 map Rotri .
 map mermin .
 map . etthil merch .
  *cinnan . [*fo. 193b,
       col. 1.]
 map . rotri .

---

 1 The final *n* of this word written above the line.
 2 A letter (*i*) was written, and afterwards erased, between the *p* and *ſ* of this contraction, both here and under the years 809, 840, and 944.
 3 The final *d* altered from a prior *t*. 4 Read *iugulatuſ*.
 5 Read *Catguocaun*. 6 This *a* added above the line.
 7 The second *l* terminates in an unusual flourish (?) which makes it not very unlike a *b*.

map . Iutguaul .

map . Catgualart .

map . Catgollau*n* .

map . Cat man[1].

map . Iacob .

map . Beli .

map . Run .

map . Mailcun .

map . Catgolau*n* .

Iauhir[2].

map . Eniau*n* girt .

map . Cuneda .

map . Æte*rn* .

map . Pate*rn* . peſrut .

map . Tacit .

map . Cein .

map . Guoɪcein .

map doli .

map . Guoɪdoli .

map . ðumn .

map . Gurdu*mn*[3].

map . Amguoloẏt .

map . A*n*guerit[4].

map . Oumu*n* .

map . ðubun .

map . Brithguein .

map . Eugein .

map . Aballac .

map . Amalech[5]. q*ui* fuit .

beli magni filiuſ .

et anna mater eiuſ .

qua*m* dic*un*t . eſſe[6].

[conſo-

brina MARIÆ

uirginiſ . mat*ri*ſ .

d'ni n'ri ih'u xp'i .

---

[1] Read *Catman*.   [2] This is a mistake for *Lauhir*.

[3] The natural reading of the contraction would make the word "Gurdu*n*" or "Gurdu*m*", but "Gurdu*mn*" was probably meant, and is certainly right.

[4] As far as the contraction goes, this might be read either "Amguerit" or "A*n*guerit". The name is spelt with an *m* in *Cott. Vesp. A*, xiv, fo. 70ᵇ (= *Cambro-British Saints*, p. 144) ; but with an *n* in the same MS., fo. 37ᵇ (= *C.-B. SS.*, p. 82, § 44), and in No. VI of the Jesus College Pedigrees.

[5] This *Amalech* is omitted in No. x (*infra*), and is probably a mere *doublet* of *Aballac*, now *Afallach*, a form of which the correctness is amply attested. In this genealogy, as given in *Cott. Vesp. A.* xiv, fo. 37ᵇ, *Báállad* (a misreading for *Aballach*) stands in the place of our *Aballac*, and *Aballach* in that of our *Amalech*.

[6] The two *e*'s of the usual contraction for "*esse*" have each the mark underneath which makes *e* into the character used for *æ*. This is at least unusual, but is found elsewhere in our MS., and also (*e.g.*) in *Cott. Vesp. A.*, xiv, fo. 86ᵃ, in the contractions for "*esset*" and "*essent*".

[II.]

[Ⓞ]uein . map . elen . merc .
Ioumarc[1]. map . Hime-
ẏt .

[col. 2.]

map . Tancoyflt .
    merc . ouein .
map . marget iut[2].
map . Teudof .
map . Regin .
map . Catgocaun .
map . Cathen .
map . Cloten[3].
map . Nougoẏ .
map . Arthur .
map . Petr .
map . Cincar .
map . Guoꝛtepir .
map . Aircol .
map . Triphun .

map . Clotri .
map . Gloitguin[4].
map . Nimet .
map . ꝺimet .
map . Maxim gulecic[5].
map . Protec .
map . Protectoꝛ .
map Ebiud .
map . Eliud .
map . Stater .
map . Pincr miffer .
map . Couftanf .
map . Conftanti-
    ni magni .
map . Conftantíí[6]
    et helen . lu-
    ic dauc[7]. q*ue*
    de brittan-
    nia exiuit .

[1] Read L*oumarc*.   [2] Read *margetiut*.
[3] This *Cloten* is omitted in No. XV, *q. v.*, where *Cathen* is made the
son of *Nougoy* (usually called *Noë ab Arthur*).
[4] A mistake for *Cloitguin*. This is Clydwyn, the son of Brychan
Brycheiniog, whose reputed conquest of Demetia has caused him to
to be foisted into this Demetian pedigree. *Nimet* was his son, not
his father, and appears as *Neufedd* in the Breconshire pedigrees. In
No. IV (*infra*) he is made into *Eidinet*, and made the *grand*son of
Maxen Wledig; whilst in *Bonedd Gwyr y Gogledd* this *Eidinet* has
been manufactured into the Welsh name *Ednyfed*, which could never
have been spelt *Eidinet*, and in the orthography of our MS. is spelt
Iutnimet, a form occurring in No. XVIII, *infra*.
[5] Read *guletic*.
[6] First written *Constrantii*, and the *r* subsequently expuncted. The
a was also expuncted, but the expuncting dot subsequently smudged
away by the scribe.
[7] Read *luitdauc*, which might stand equally well for (the modern)
lwythog or *lwyddog*. *Luidt* for *llwyth* occurs in *B. of St. Chad*, p. 141.

ad cruce*m* xp'i
querenda*m* u*f*q*ue*
ad ier*ufa*lem . *et* in-
de attulit fe-
cu*m* u*f*q*ue* adcon-

[col. 3.] *f*tantinopoli*n* . *et eft*
[ibi
u*f*q*ue* inhodiernu*m*
[die*m* .
[III.]
[**H**]iguel . map . caratauc .
map . meriaun .
map . rumaun .
map . Enniaun .
map . Ẏtigoẏ .
map . Cat gual[1] . cri*f*ban .
map . Cangan .
map . Meic .
maᵽ . Cingla*f* .
map . Eugein . dant guin .
map . Enniaun . girt .
map   cuneda .
[IV.]
[**Ḧ**]ud gual .
map   Tutagual   .
map   Anarant[2]   .
map   Mermin   .
map   Anthec   .

map   Tutagual   .
map   Run   .
map   Neithon   .
map   Senill   .
map   Dinacat   .
map   Tutagual   .
map   Eidinet[3]   .
map   Anthun   .
map   Maxim gule-
tic q*ui* occidit
gratianu*m* rege*m*
romanorum .
[V.]
[**R**]un[4] map arth
gal .
map   Du*m*nagual .
map   Riderch .
map   Eugein
map   Du*m*nagual .
*map . Teudebur .   [*fo. 194ᵃ,
map . Beli .   col. 1.]
map . Elfin .
map . Eugein .
map . Beli .
map . Neithon .
map . Guipno[5] .
map . Du*mn* gual[6] .
hen .
map . Cinuit .

[1] Read *Catgual;* and so in similar cases.   [2] Read *Anaraut.*
[3] See note on *Gloitguin, supra,* in No. II.
[4] In the space where the rubric *R* should be, a small *r* is inserted
in a hand not much later than the MS.
[5] Certainly a mistake for *Guipno* (= *Gwyddno*).
[6] See note on *Gurdumn* in No. I, which is similarly applicable here.

map . Ceritic gu-
    letic .
map . Cẏnloẏp .
map . Cinhil .
map . Cluim .
map . Curſalen[1].
map . Fer .
map . Confer ip-
    ſe *eſt* uero
    olitauc .
    dimoꝛ . me-
    ton[2]. uendi-
    tuſ . eſt .
[VI.]
[R]iderch hen .
map . Tutagual .
map . Clinoch .
map . Dum gual .
    hen .

[VII.]
[C]linog[3] eitin .
map . Cinbelim[4].
map . Dumn gual[5] hen .
[VIII.]
[U]rb gen[6].
map . Cinmarc .
map . Merchia-
    num[7].
map . Gurguſt .
map . Coilhen[8].
[IX.]
[G]uallauc .
map . Laenauc .
*map . Maſguic .   [*col. 2.]
    clop .
map . Ceneú .
map . Coẏl . hen .

[1] Or "Cursalem"? In Geoffrey of Monmouth's "History", Book ix, chap. 12, the name is so spelt, according to the copy in *Royal MS*. 13, D. V., fo. 28ᵇ, col. 2.

[2] These three Welsh words are of unknown meaning. Mr. Skene's rendering of the first by "rich" is impossible, for the word he was thinking of would necessarily be written *guolutauc* at the date of the MS. Doubtless the word is an epithet; and the other two words *might* mean "to the Mediterranean (literally, 'the middle') sea." Or *mor* may be the common man's name *Mor*, and *meton* the same as the last part of the epithet *Muighmhedhuin*, in *Annals of the Four Masters*, under A.D. 365.

[3] Is not this a mistake for *Clitnoy* (the person now called *Clydno Eiddin*)? *Clinoch* (just above) must be meant for the name now spelt *Clynog*, which never could have been spelt with a final *g* in the 10th—12th centuries.   [4] Read *Cinbelin*.

[5] See note on *Dumngual* in No. v (*supra*) and note there referred to.

[6] Read *Urbgen* (now *Urien*).   [7] Read *merchiaun*.

[8] *Map Ceneu* is omitted between this line and the preceding one by the scribe of the MS. See No. XII *infra*, and note on *let lum* there.

[x.]

[𝔐]orcant .

map . Coledauc .

map . Morcant .

bulc .

map . Cincar

braut .

map[1] . Branhen .

map . ẟumngual[2].

moilmut .

map . Garbani

aún[3].

map . Coẏl hen .

map[4]. Guote p auc .

map . Tec ma-

. nt[5].

map . Teu-

hant .

map . Telpu-

. il .

map . Vrb

an .

map . Grat .

map . Iume-

tel .

map . Riti-

girn .

map . Oude-

cant .

map . . Ou-

tigir[6].

map . Ebiud .

map . Eudof .

map . Eudelen .

map . Aballac[7].

map . Beli . et

anna .

[xi.]

[𝔇]unaut .

*map . pappo .   [*col. 3.]

map . Ceneu .

map . Coẏlhen .

[1] *Braut Bran hen probably* means "brother to Brân hên" ; if so this *map* should be cancelled.

[2] See notes on this name under Nos. v and vii, and the note referred to in the first of them.

[3] The acute accent is over the final *n*, but presumably meant for the *u*. See note on *Selemiaun*, end of No. xxvii *infra*.

[4] This *map* should of course be cancelled. *Guotepauc* (now *Godebog*), is Cunedda's epithet. He should rightly be called " Coel *Odebog*", not " Coel *Godebog*", as he usually is.

[5] Read *Tecmant* (now *Tegfan*). The last part of this word is in the MS. in the same line as the following *Teu-*, from which the preposed stop is intended to mark it off. Similarly, *-il*, a little lower down, is in the same line with *Vrb-*.

[6] Read *Outigirn* (now *Eudeýrn*) ; and cf. *Cattegir*, end of No. xxvii *infra*, and note thereon.

[7] See note on *Amalech*, end of No. i (*supra*).

[xii.]

[**G**]urci . ha .

peret*ur* me pion[1].

eleuther . caſ cord .

maur .

map . let lum[2] .

map . Ceneú .

map . Coẏlhen .

[xiii.]

[**T**]riphu*n* .

map . regin .

map . morgetiud .

map . Teudoſ .

map . regin[3].

[xiv.]

[**R**]egin . iu don .

iOuem[4]. Treſ filíí .

morgetiud . ſu*nt* .

[xv.]

[**G**]ripiud . Teudoſ

caten . Treſ ſu*nt*

filíí nougoẏ .

et ſanant elized[5].

filia illor*um*[6]. mat*er*

[erat

regiſ pouiſ .

[xvi.]

[**R**]un . map . neithon .

map . Caten .

map . Caurta*m* .

map . Sergua*n* .

map . Leta*n*[7].

---

[1] Read *mepion.* This Welsh sentence means : "Gwrgi and Peredur (were) the sons of Eliffer *Gosgordd fawr* ('of the great retinue')".

[2] This should be "Gurguft *letlum*" (now called *Gwrwst ledlwm*). See No. viii (*supra*) and last note thereon.

[3] For this and the two following genealogies cf. No. ii. (*supra*), and our note on *Cloten* there.

[4] Read *Ouein,* as his name is rightly given in fo. 193ᵇ, col. 2, line 2, *supra* (No. ii). The scribe, having first written *Ouem,* afterwards prefixed a small *i* to the word, perhaps under the impression that the name ought to be that now spelt *Ieuaf,* but in Old-Welsh *Iouab,* and permissibly *Iouam.*

[5] This word's proper place is after *erat,* at the end of the next line. Evidently in the original MS. the word ended a line, and was crowded out of it so as to be placed in the line above, with a mark referring it to its proper place ; and the omission of a scribe to notice this mark led to the misplacement of the word. Elisse (to whose memory the Valle Crucis pillar was set up) was King of Powys about 700—750 ; and Sannan verch Noë ab Arthur was his mother.

[6] This should of course be *illius, i.e.,* of *Nougoy.*

[7] Or "Letam" ?

map . Catleú .

map . Catel .

map . decion .

map . Cinif fcaplaut[1].

map . Louhen[2].

map . Guid gen .

map . Caratauc .

map . Cinbelin[3].

map . Teuhant .

map . Conftantif .

map Conftantini   .

      magni[4]   .

map Conftantini   .

map Galerii   .

map Diocletiani q*ui* p*er*

      fecutu*f*[4] eft xp'ia-

      nof[4] toto mundo .

      Inte*m*pore illiu*f* paf-

fi funt beati mar-

tiref inbrittannia .

Albanuf . Iulianu*f* .

Aron . cu*m* aliif com-

pluribu*f*   .

map Caroci[5]   .

map Probi   .

map Titti   .

map Auriliani   .

map Antun . ðu . &

      cleopatre   .

map Valeriani   .

map Galli   .

map Deciu*f* . muf   .

map Philippuf   .

map Gordianu*f*   .

map Alaximu*f*[6]   .

map Alaxander   .

---

[1] The *a* of this word may *perhaps* be read an *o*. It seems to have been begun as an *a*, and finished as an *o*. Geoffrey of Monmouth (Book ix, chapter 12) has a *Masgoit clof*laut, according to some MSS. (*e.g.*, *Royal MS.* 13, D. V., fo. 28ᵇ, col. 2, cited above) whose epithet must contain the same vocable as our *scaplaut;* and indeed the personage would seem to be but a hybrid concoction from *Masguic clop* (= "M. the lame") of our No. IX (*supra*), and this *Cinis scaplaut.*

[2] Or "Louhe*m*"? But possibly *Lou hen* is meant to = the Middle-Welsh *Lleu hen.*

[3] Or "Cinbeli*m*", which occurs *supra*, in No. VII.

[4] *Map* was written at the beginnings of these three lines in its proper column, and then erased.

[5] This word is marginally glossed "í. ímper*ator*íf" in a later hand.

[6] We have not compared this marvellous list of the Roman Emperors with their real history, but are led by the very peculiar inclination of the *Al-* of this word to suspect that it *may* have been originally copied from a large Roman *M*. Quite a different *M* is used in this MS. Perhaps, however, the name is a cross between *Maximus* and *Alexius.*

map	Aurilianuſ	.	map	Claudiuſ	
map	Mapmau cannuſ	.	map	Tiberiuſ ſub	
map	Antoniuſ	.		quo paſſuſ eſt .	
map	Seueruſ	.		dn'ſ n'r ih'c x'pc	
map	Moebuſ	.		Octauianuſ³ au-	
map	Commodiuſ	.		guſti ceſſariſ .	
map	Antoniuſ	.		Intempore il-	
map	Adiuuanduſ	.		liuſnatuſ eſt	
map	Troianuſ¹	.		d'nſ n'r ih'ſ xp'c	
map	Nero ſub quo	.		[XVII.]	
	paſſi² ſunt bea-	.	[C]uhelm⁴ map bleẏ-		
	ti apoſtoli d'ni n'ri .			diud	.
	ih'u xp'i PETRI .	.	map	Caratauc	.
[col. 2.]	& PAVli .		map	Iouanaul⁵	.
map	Domitianuſ	.	map	Eiciaun	.
map	Tituſ	.	map	B rochmail⁶	.
map	Veſpaſſianuſ	.	map	Ebiau⁷	.

¹ Clumsily altered into *Traianuſ, possibly* by the scribe.

² Some word (evidently *map*) was written, immediately below the *map* of the last line, in this line and the two following ones, and then completely scratched out.

³ *Map* has certainly been omitted before this word, and *map* or *filius* after it. The *-ſa-* of *ceſſariſ* is a peculiar "conjoint" character.

⁴ This should almost certainly be *Cuhelin*, but we think that an *m* must be read in the MS.

⁵ The *I* is a hybrid between *I* and *l*: probably *I* is meant. The person is called *Iewana6l* in *J. C. MS.* 20, No. XL.

⁶ The *h* is expressed by the regular *Irish* contraction, somewhat resembling a T on its side (thus, ⊢) over the *c*.

⁷ This name (here and twice below), should almost certainly be *Ebiaun,* now *Eifion.* In the corresponding genealogy of Dunoding in *J. C. MS.* 20 (No. XL: see p. 62, below), it is spelt, in the order of its occurrence, *Eidan, Einya6n,* and *eina6n,* respectively; of which the last two are miscopied from *Eiuya6n* and *eiua6n,* the Middle-Welsh forms of O.-W. *Ebiaun,* and the first from M.-W. *Eidaun,* equivalent to *Eiuaun.* The person meant by the earliest

map	Popdelgu[1]	.	map . Iutnimet .	
map	Popgen	.	map . Egeniud .	
map	Iſaac	.	map . Brocmail	.
map	Ebiau	.	map Sualda .	.
map	Mouric	.	map Iudris[3].	.
map	Dinacat	.	map Gueinoth[4].	.
map	Ebiau	.	map Glitnoth .	.
map	Dunaut	.	map Guurgint[5].	
map	Cuneda	.	*barmb truch .	[*col. 3.]
	[XVIII.]		map Gatgulart[6].	.
[ℭ]inan[2] map			map Meriaun	.
brochmail		.	map Cuneda[7]	.

Ebiau(n) is undoubtedly the prince of that name from whom is derived the territorial name *Eifionydd*, often called *Eidyonyd* (= *Eiddionydd*) in Middle-Welsh.   Eifionydd and Ardudwy together made up the *Cantref* ("hundred of") *Dunoding*, so called from Dunod ab Cunedda, so that this Eifion was naturally made to be (and perhaps was) his son.

¹ This name and the following are represented by *Hoedle6* and *Podgen hen* respectively in *J. C. MS.* 20, No. XL, which makes one suppose that the second *p* in both words may be miscopied from a þ.

² In the space where the capital initial of this word should be, *map* has been written and then erased.

³ The *s* of this word is written over the line, being substituted for an expuncted *t*.

⁴ This is almost certainly a mistake for *Gueithno*. Both *Gueinoth* and *Glitnoth* are represented by *one* person, *Gweidno*, in *J. C. MS.* 20, No. XLI, and *Gweiddno* is a bye-form of *Gwyddno*. *Glitnoth* is suspiciously like a *doublet* of *Gueinoth*, and itself seems a mistake for *Guithno*, the modern *Gwyddno*.

⁵ This the regular Old-Welsh form of the name now spelt *Gwrin*, whence *Llanwrin*.   *Gwrin farfdrwch* was made by Geoffrey of Monmouth into one of his series of fabulous British kings, under the name of *Gurgiunt barbtruc*, from whom in turn later Welsh antiquaries have evolved a still more mythical *Gwrgant farfdrwch*. *Gwrgan(t)* in Old-Welsh is *Gurcant*, not *Gurgint* (or *Guurgint*).

⁶ Read *Catgualart*, or perhaps *Catgualatr*.

⁷ The words *mub Typiaun* are omitted between this and the previous line. See No. XXXII, and note on *Typi(p)aun* there.

[XIX.]

[C]atguallaun liu   .

map   Guitcun   .

map   Samuil penniffel . .

map   Pappo poſl priten .

map   Ceneu   .

map   Gŷl[1] hen   .

[XX.]

[?I]mor[2] map moriud .

map   Ædan   .

map   Mor   .

map   Brechiaul   .

[XXI.]

[M]eriaun map

[loudogu .

[XXII.]

[S]elim . map Cinan[3] .

map   Brocmaẏl   .

map   Cincen[3]   .

map   Maucanu[4]   .

map   Pafcent   .

map . Catte girn[5]   .

map   Catel dunlurc[6] .

---

[1] Read *Coyl*, and compare this genealogy with No. XI, *supra*.

[2] *J. C. MS.* 20, No. XLVI, gives this name as "*Amor*". We know nothing of him or when he lived, and regard the conversion of his ancestor *Brechiaul* (= *Breichiol*), by the *J. C. MS.* genealogist into a "*Brochwael ab* Cunedda Wledig" as a mistake.

[3] See No. XXVII, *infra*, where these two names are wrongly transposed, and our note on them there.

[4] Read *Maucann*, or perhaps *Maucant* : probably the former. Cf. the mistake *gurhaiernu* in No. XXIII, *infra*, and note thereon, and *linhenlanú* for *linhenlann* in Rhygyfarch's *Life of St. David* (Cott. Vesp. A., xiv, fo. 61ª), miscopied *Linhenlanum* in *Cambro-British Saints*, p. 117.

[5] Read *Cattegirn*. "Nennius" makes this *Catteẏrn* son to Vortigern (*S.*, § 44, 48), and later pedigree-makers have tortured his name into *Cyndeẏrn*. In the preceding *map* some letter has been begun, and left unerased and uncancelled, before the *p*.

[6] This well-known epithet is spelt *durnluc* elsewhere in this MS. (in *Nennius*, fo. 181ª, l. 12 = *S.*, § 35), for which we believe *dunlurc* is a mistake. For such an insertion of *r* from another syllable, cf. (Cair) *urnarc*, in the *Catalogue of Cities*, *infra*, certainly for *C. urnac*, i.e., *Caer Urnach*. Were *durnluc* for *Deyrnllwg*, it would certainly be spelt *Tigirn-* or *Tegirn-(l)luc* at the date of our MS., whilst *Durn-* or *Turn-* would at all times have been (as it now is) an impossible orthography for *Teyrn*, nor would the initial mutation from *t* to *d* incident to "epithets" have been expressed in the orthography of our MS. He is called *Cadell deyrlloch* in *J. C. MS.* 20, No. XVIII, and *C. deernlluc* (the last certainly = *deyrnllwg* or *-llug*) in No. XVI. See our note on the epithet in *Y Cymmrodor*, vol. vii, p. 119.

[XXIII.]

[?] effelif . map gur
haiernu¹

map	Elbodgu .
map	Cinnin .
map	Millo .
map	Camuir .
map	Brittu .
map	Cattegirn .
map	Catell .

⌈XXIV.⌉

[Ƨ]elim . map iouab .

map	Guit gen² .
map	Bodug .
map	Canantinail³ .
map	Cerennior .
map	Ermic .
map	Ecrin .

[XXV.)

[Ỻ]udnerth map .

[morgen .

[fo. 195ᵃ,   . map   Catgur .
col. 1.]

. map	Catmor .
. map	Merguid .
. map	Moriutned . .
. map	Morhen .
. map	Morcant .
. map	Botan .
. map	Morgen .
. map	Mormaẏl .
. map	Glaft . unu*m*

funt . glaftenic⁴.

qui uener*unt* q*ue*

uocat*ur* . loẏt

coẏt .

[XXVI.]

[Ǥ]uocaun .

. map	Mouric .
. map	Du*m*ngual-
	laun .
. map	Arthgen .
. map	Seiffil .
. map	Clitauc .
. map	Artgloys .

¹ Read *Gurhaiern*n.   ² Read *Guitgen*.

³ This is undoubtedly a mistake in transcribing *Carant*m*ail* from a "Hiberno-Saxon" hand. The second stroke of the first *n* of *Canantinail* is not carried quite to the bottom of the line, and it is possible that the scribe in making it was attempting roughly to copy the original *r*. The most remarkable *n* of this sort in the MS. is that of *dunlurc*, end of No. XXII, *supra*.

⁴ *Glastenic* is certainly the native name of Glastonbury, from Cornish and Breton *Glasten* or *Glastan* "oaks", *not* (as is often given in dictionaries) "ilexes or holm-oaks", those trees not being indigenous in these latitudes. (*Cair*) *loyt coyt* (see below), has been brilliantly identified by Mr. H. Bradley with *Letocetum* (now *Lichfield*). The whole sentence is dislocated and defective. Can the *unū fl*' of the MS. be a mistake for *un̄ eft* (= *unde est*)?

. map	Artboᵭgu	.	map	Cincen³	.
. map	Boᵭgu	.	map	Brocmail	.
. map	Serguil	.	map	Cinan³	.
. map	Iufaẏ	.	*map	Maucant	. [*col. 2.]
. map	Ceretic	.	map	Pafcent	.
. map	Cuneda .	.	map	Cattegir⁴	.
	[xxvii.]		map	Catel	.
. map¹[ℭ]incen .			map⁵	Selemiaun .	
map	Catel	.		[xxviii.]	
map	Brocmaẏl .		[Ḫ]uᵭ hail⁶		.
map	Elitet²	.	map	Atroẏs	.
map	Guilauc	.	map	Fernmail	.
map	Eli	,	map	Iudhail	.
map	Eliud	.	map	Morcant	.

¹ This *map* is wrongly inserted.

² Read *Elizet*. The stock "antiquaries' form", *Eliseg*, can only arise from someone's having misread on the Valle Crucis pillar erected to Elisse's memory a "Hiberno-Saxon" *t* as the very similar *g*. The final letter of the name was more regularly written *d*, as in Nos. xv, xxx, and xxxi, and was sounded like the *dd* of modern Welsh; it is omitted in the modern pronunciation of the name. Such forms as *Elissau*, etc., are but the "restorations" (from *Elisse*) of genealogists bent on blazoning their own ignorance of the past.

³ These two names have been transposed. There is no doubt that Cyngen was the *father*, Cynan (Garwyn) the *son*, of Brochwel (Ysgythrog).

⁴ Read *Cattegirn* ; and cf. *Outigir* at end of No. x *supra*, and the *Cadegyr* of the Triads.

⁵ If *Selemiaun* = the modern *Selyfion*, the name of an (unknown) district derived from one Selyf (? Selyf sarffgadau ap Cynan Garwyn, whose genealogy is given in No. xxii, *supra*), and appended epithetically to Cadell "Deyrnllwg" as having ruled over it, this *map* should be cancelled. But it *may* be a man's name from some such Low-Latin name as *Solymianus*, as *Garbaniaun* (in No. x *supra*), also called *Garmonyaón*, is probably from *Germanianus*, though that too may be a territorial or tribal designation derived from one Garmon or Germanus.

⁶ Read *Iudhail*.

map	Atroyſ	.	cen³. filíí broc-	.
map	Teudubric¹	.	mail . filíí elized	.
	[xxix.]		[xxxii.]	
	[**B**]rocmail	.	[**H**]ec ſunt nomi-	.
map	Mouric	.	na filioru*m* cune-	.
map	Artmail	.	da quor*um* nume-	.
map	Riſ	.	ru*ſ* erat . ix . Tẏ-	.
map	Iudhail	.	pipaun⁴ *primo*-	.
map	Morcant	.	genitu*ſ* . qu*i*mo*ȝt*u-	.
	[xxx.]		u*ſ* inregione q*ue*	.
	[**M**]aun ar-		uocat*ur* manaú	.
	tan iouab		guodotin . *et* n*o*n	.
	meic . filíí grippi²		uenit huc cu*m*	.
	filíí elized	.	patre ſuo *et* cu*m*	.
	[xxxi.]		f*r*atribu*ſ* ſuiſ . pre⁵	.
	[**E**]lized ioab	.	*meriaun . filiu*ſ* eiu*ſ* .	[*col. 3.]
	ædan . filíí cin-	.	diuiſit poſſeſſioneſ	

¹ *Map Mouric* is certainly omitted between this and the preceding line.

² This word is unfinished. There has been omitted at this point : "-ud filii cincen filii catel(l) filii brocmail". See No. xxvii *supra*, and for Gruffudd and Elisse, sons of Cyngen, see *Annales Cambriæ*, under 814. Gruffudd seems to have been left out of the following pedigree on account of his early death.

³ The words "filii catel(l)" have been omitted after "cincen". The exact agreement of Cyngen ab Cadell's pedigree up to Gwylog (or Gwyllog ?), as given here (in No. xxvii *supra*) with the same as given on the Valle Crucis pillar, *set up by Cyngen himself*, places this part of the princely pedigree of Powys beyond a shadow of a doubt. It is worth noting that there are omissions as serious as those here and in No. xxx to be found in the same portion of the same pedigree, as given in a sixteenth-century MS., *Harl.* 3325, where at fo. 142ᵇ Cadell and Brochwel are omitted between Cyngen and Elisse.

⁴ Certainly a mistake for *Typiaun* (now Tybion), but the superfluous *p may* have been miscopied from a *y*, pronounced as a semivowel.

⁵ Apparently this word is incomplete, and meant for *predictis*, as pointed out by Sir S. Meyrick.

inter fratreſ ¹. ſuoſ . ii..   [ℭ]air . ligualid   .

Oſmail . iii . rumaun . iiii.   [ℭ]air me guaiδ .

δunaut . v . Ceretic . vi .   [ℭ]air . colun

abloyc . vii . enniaun . girt .   [ℭ]air . ebrauc

viii . δocmail . ix . etern .   [ℭ]air . cuſtoeint

[XXXIII.]   [ℭ]air caratauc

[𝕳]ic *eſt terminuſ* eorum   [ℭ]air . grauth

[aſſumine   [ℭ]air . maunguid

quod uocatur dubr duiú .   [ℭ]air . lundem³

[uſ-   [ℭ]air . ceint

que ad aliud flumen tebi .   [ℭ]air . guiragon

[et   [ℭ]air . periſ

tenuerunt plurimaſ re-   [ℭ]air daun

[gioneſ   [ℭ]air legion

in occidentali plaga brit-   [ℭ]air . guricon

tanniæ .   [ℭ]air . ſegeint

[CATALOGUE OF CITIES.]   [ℭ]air . legeion guar uſic⁴   .

[𝕳]æc² ſunt nomina omnium   [ℭ]air . guent   .

ciuitatum . que ſunt in   [ℭ]air . brithon   . [fo. 195 .]

[tota brit-   [ℭ]air . lerion

tannia . quarum numeruſ   [ℭ]air δraitoú   .

[eſt xxviii.   [ℭ]air Penſa uel coẏt   .

[ℭ]air guorthigirn .   [ℭ]air urnarc⁵   .

[ℭ]air . guinntguic .   [ℭ]air celemion   ,

[ℭ]air . mincip .   [ℭ]air luit coẏt   .

[Here follows in the MS. the tract *De Mirabilibus Britan-niæ* (printed in Stevenson's *Nennius*, pp. 56—62, §§ 67—76) with which conclude the additions to the *Historia Britonum.*]

¹ There is a superfluous mark of contraction (probably meant to stand for -*er*-) over the *t* of this word.

² The capital has been filled in by a much later hand.

³ Read *lundein*.   ⁴ Read *uiſc*.

⁵ Read *urnac*, and cf. *dunlurc* at end of No. XXII *supra*, and note thereon. Stevenson (p. 62) wrongly makes the MS. read *urnac*.

PEDIGREES FROM JESUS COLLEGE MS. 20.*

[I.] [Fo. 33ª]—Llyma r mod y treythir o ach kyna6c sant.
[1.] Kyna6c mab brachan M. chormuc M. eurbre g6ydel o
iwedon. Mam vrachan oed Marchell merch te6dric. M. teid-
fallt. M. teidtheryn. M. thathal. M. ann6n du vrenhin groec.
[II.]—Enweu y meibyon ereill y brachan. [2.] Drem dremrud.
M. brachan. [3.] Clytwin. M. brachan. Clyta6c sant.
Hedetta sant meibyon clytwin. [4.] [A]ttlien. M. brachan.
[5.] Papai. M. brachan. [6.] Kynon Mab brachan. [7.]
Runañ. M. brachan yssyd yny a elwir Mana6. [8.] Mar-
charairjun. ygkeueilya6c. [9.] Dindat M brachan yn llan
ymdyfri. Pascen M dingat. Cyblider. M. dingat. [10.] Ber-
win. M. brachan ygkerny6. [11.] Reidoc M. brachan yn
freink. yny lle a elwir t6mbreidoc oe en6 ef. [III.]—Llyma
enweu Merchet brachan weithon. [1.] G6ladus verch
vrachan. Mam catt6c sant. [2.] Argīgen verch brachan.
g6reic Ioroereth hirblant. [3.] Marchell verch brachan g6reic
g6rhynt bramdrut. [4.] Tutlith verch vrachan. yn [Fo. 33ᵇ]
llys ron6y ygwlat vorgan. [5.] Drynwin verch vrachan. mam
vryen. Erduduyl g6yñdorliud. Owein. M. vryen. A Morud
Verch vryen. G6rgi a pheredur ac arthur penuchel. a tonlut. a
hortnan. a dyrnell. trydyth gwyn dorliud. [6.] Kyngar verch
vrachan. [7.] Rinhidyr verch vrachan. [8.] [M]eleri verch
vrachan. gwreic keredic. man sant. tat dewi. [9.] G6wa6r
verch vrachan. [10.] Gutuyl verch vrachan g6reic kynger
mab kynwa6r. a mam brochuael yscithra6c. a mam veic
meng6rac. a man sanant gwreic vaelg6n. [11.] [G]rugon
verch vrachan. gwreic Katra6t vrenhin. [12.] [K]erdech

* Reprinted from Y Cymmrodor 8 (1887) 83–92

v*erch* vrachan yssyd yglan tywi ymeiryonyd. [13.] 𝕮agh-
6ystyl. [14.] 𝕿utuel v*erch* vra*chan*. ym m*er*thyr. [15.]
𝕲oleudyd gwreic tutwa6l beper. [16.] [𝕷l]van v*erch*
vra*chan* ho̅no̅ oed vam aidan mab gwauream vrada6c. [17.]
Gwen̄ v*erch* vra*chan*. yn talgard. [18.] 𝕱elis v*erch* vra*chan*.
[19.] 𝕿ebieu v*erch* vra*chan* yn estratewi. [20.] [𝕶]em-
breith v*erch* vrachan. [21.] 𝕽yn-[Fo. 34ᵃ]eidon v*erch*
vra*chan*. ygkitweli ymynyd kyuor. [22.] 𝕮ledei v*erch*
vra*chan*. yn emlyn. [23.] 𝕲wen̄ v*erch* vrachan ymon vam
gymry. [24.] 𝕷lud verch vra*chan* yn ruthun yg6lat vor-
gant.

[IV.]—𝕳𝖞𝖒𝖆 𝖜𝖊𝖎𝖙𝖍𝖔𝖓 𝖆𝖈𝖍 𝕮𝖆𝖙𝖙6𝖈 𝖘𝖆𝖓𝖙.

𝕮att6c. M gwynlli6. M. gli6s. M. filur. M. Nor. M. ab
𝕺wein. M*ab* maxen. Maxen wledic brenhin y brytanyeit. a
gwedy hyn̄y yn Amhera6dyr yn rufein. A chynan yn
v*ren*hin yny le. Kynan. M. eudaf. M. Custenin. M. Maxen.
M. Maximian*us*. M. Constantin*us*. M. Custeint. Mam Constantin*us* oed elen luedya6c. yr hon a enilla6d y groes ygkar-
usalem. Ac a duc ran̄ genthi y gonstantinobyl. A ran arall a
anuones yr brytanyeit. Ac y gyt a hi yd oed ewein ymab.
ewein oed vab y vaxen. o keindrech verch. Reiden. Reiden.
M. eledi. M. mordu. M. meircha6n. M. Kasswalla6n. yn
amser y kasswalla6n [Fo. 34ᵇ] h6n̄6 y kymella6d y rufeinwyr
treth o ynys prydein. 𝕶aswalla6n. M. beli ma6r. M. Anna.
yr anna hon̄ oed verch y amhera6dyr rufein. yr anna ho̅no̅ a
dywedei wyr yr eifft y bot yn gyfynnithder6 y veir vor6yn.
[V.]—𝕮𝖊𝖓𝖜𝖊𝖚 𝖒𝖊𝖎𝖇𝖔𝖓. Ewein vab keredic. Pedroc sant.
Kynvarch. Edelic. Luip. Clesoeph. Sant. Perun. Saul. Peder.
Katwaladyr. Meirchya6n. G6rrai. Mur. Margam Amroeth.
G6her. Cornuill. Catwall. Cetweli. Ac vn verch. Don6n.
g6reic meur*ic* mab emminni. merch. Kynvarch. M. meircha6n.
M. g6rgust letl6m. M*ab*. Cene6. M. Coyl hen. M. godeba6c.
M. tecwant. M. Eweint. M. tep6yll. M. Vrban. M. Grad. M.
K6nedyl. M. Kndeern. M. Tegant. M. Kyndeern wledic. M.

elud. M. eudos. M. eudolen. M. auallach. M. aphlech. M. Beli ma6r. vab. anna. val y mae vchot.

[VI.] [Fo. 35ᵃ]—𝕮uneda. M. Edern. M. Padarn beisrud. M. tegyth. M. Iago. M. geneda6c. M. Cein. M. Gorein. M. Doli. M. G6rdoli. M. D6fyn. M. Gordofyn. M. Anuueret. M. eimet. M. Dibun. M. Prydein. M. Ewein. M. Auallach. M. Amalech. M. Beli. M. Anna. val y dewetp6yt vchot.

[VII.]—𝕮Ebia6n. ym. Meiria6n meirioñyd. Run. Rywin-nya6c. Duna6t. yn dunodyn. Ceredic. ygkeredigya6n. Afloch. yn aphlocya6n. Einya6n hyrth. Docuayl. ygkeueilya6c. Edern. yn Edreinya6n. D6y verchet Cuneda. Tecgygyl. A Gweñ. g6reic. Anla6d wledic. Mam veibyon Cuneda. oed wa6l verch Coyl hen. G6reic Coyl hen oed verch Gadeon. M. Eudaf hen. vchot.

[VIII.]—𝕮E6d6r. M. Griffri. M. Elisse. M. the6d6r. M. Gruffud. Gruffud. a the6dos. [Fo. 35ᵇ] a cathen. Meibyon y vrenhin powys. o sanant *verch* elisse y mam. Elisse. *verch* neuue hen mab te6d6r. M. rein. M. Cad6ga6n. M. Caden. M. Keindrec. Merch. rualla6n. M. Idwalla6n. M. Llowarch. M. Rigeneu. M. Rein dremrud. M. brach*an*. val y mae vchot.

[IX.]—𝕸organt. M. Eweint. M. howel. M. Rees. M. Aruael. M. G6ryat. M. Brochuael. M. Rees. M. Nud hael. M. Morgant. M. Adroes. M. Meuric. M. the6dric. M. Llywarch. M. Nynnya6. M.¹ Erb. M. Erbic. M. meuric. M. Enenni. verch. Erbic. M. meur*i*c. M. Carada6c vreich vras. O en6 Morgant vchot y gelwir Morgañ6c. Ereill a

¹ On the margin, just below the line beginning with this word, the following sentence, written in a later and very ornate hand of the 15th century, is commenced, and continued to the bottom of the page : " o enw Morgan mab Maglawn y kavas Morgannwg y henw: cañys Morgan wg y gelwid."

dyweit. Mae o en6. Mochteyrn predein. M. gli6s. Mal y
mae vchot.

[X.]—Morgant. M. Eweint. M. Hewel. M. Rees. M.
Arthwael. M. Kenedlon. Merch. Binael vrydic. M. llywarch.
[Fo. 36ᵃ] M. te6d6r. M. pibia6n gla6ra6c. M. Arbeth. M.
deuric sant. Merch Peibia6n. Mam theudu. M. Pedur. M.
Cado. M. Gereint M. Erbin.

[XI.]—GEreint. M. Erbin. M. Kyn6a6r. M. tudwa6l. M.
G6rwa6r. M. Gadeon M. Cynan. M. Eudaf hen. Mal y mae
vchot.   Heuyt   [XII.]—Morgant. M. Eweint. M. hoel.
M. rees. M. arthuael. M. Ceingar. Merch. Maredud. M. teudos.
o gantref teudos. Teudos. M. G6ga6n M. Cathen. M. Eleothen.
M. Nennue. M. Arthur. M. Peder.   Arthur M. Peder. M.
Kyngar. M. G6rdeber. M. Erbin. M. Aircol la6hir.

[XIII.]—Ayrcol la6hir. M. tryphun. M. Ewein vreisc. M.
Cynd6r bendigeit. M. Ewein. M. Kyngar. M. Pr6tech. M.
Ewein. M. miser. M. Custennin. M. maxen wledic. M.
Maximianus. M. Constan-[Fo. 36ᵇ]tinus ma6r. M. Custenint
o elen.

[XIV.]—Morgant mab Ewein. M. howel. M. Rees. M. y
vraustud merch gloud M. Pascen buellt. M. Gwed Gad. M.
morvo. M. Elaed. M. Pa6l. M. Idnerth. M. Riagath. M. Pascen.
M. G6rtheyrn g6rthenev.

[XV.]—G6rtheyrn g6rtheneu. M. gwida6l. M. G6doloeu.
M. gloy6 g6alltir. y g6r h6n6 a wnaeth ar ymyl hafren tref.
ac oe en6 ef y gelwir yn gaer loe6.

[XVI.]—Morgant vab Ewein. M. Howel. M. arthuael.
M. Idwal. Brodyr oedynt h6y y leuku. Lleuku merch envle6.
M. Kynfelyn. M. Iaceu. M. leuku. Merch adwent merch
Elyuer. M. Goron6y. M. Kanhaethoe. M. Ceno. M. Noe. M.
Mada6c. M. sandeph. M. tutwa6l. M. merin M. mada6c. M.
Run. M. Kenelaph drem-[Fo. 37ᵃ]rud. M. Kynan. M. kas-
anauth wledic. G6reic cassanauth wledic oed the6er merch

Bredoe. M. Kadell deernlluc. M. Cedehern. M. G6rtheyrn g6rtheneu. vchot.

[XVII.]—ℜodri ma6r. M. Meruyn vrych. M. G6rhyat. M. Elidyr. M. sandef. M. Alcun. M. tegyth. M. Ceit. M. douc. M. Llewarch hen. M. Elidyr lydanwyn. M. Meircha6n. M. G6rgust. M. Keneu. M. Coil hen. mal y mae vchot.

[XVIII.]—ℜodri ma6r mab nest. merch Cadell Pywys brenhin Pywys. Cadell m. Brochuael. M. Elisse. M. Coleda6c. M. Beli. M. Seliph. M Kynan garwin. M. Brochuael yscithra6c. M. manogan. M. Pascen M. Cadell. deyrllo :h. M. Cadern. M. G6rtheyrn g6rtheu.

[XIX.]—ℜodri ma6r. M. meruyn. M. Guriat. M. Elidyr. M. Celenion. merch tutwal [Fo. 37ᵇ] tuclith. M. Anara6d g6alchcr6n. M. meruyn ma6r. M. kyuyn. M. anllech. M. tutwa6l. M. Run. M. Neidaon. M. senilth hael. Tryd hael or gogled. Senilth. M. Dingat. M. tutwa6l. M. Edneuet. M. duna6t M. Maxen wledic. val y mae vchot.   [XX.]—Llyma enweu meibon rodri ma6r.

ℭadell. Meruyn. anara6t Aidan. Meuruc. Morgant. Nest oed y vam ef. Ac anghara *verch* oed vam y rei ereill. A deu dyn oed ida6 o wreic arall. tutwa6l. ac elisse.

[XXI.]—𝔄ngharat *verch* veuric. mab dyfa6l. M. Arthen. M. Seissill. M. Clyda6c. M. Aruodeu. M. Argloes. M. Pode6. M. Seruuel. M. Vsai. M. Keredic. M. Kuneda wledic.

[XXII.]—ℜodri. M. Meruyn. M. Ethellt. Merch Cynan tintaeth6y. M. Rodri mol6yna6c. M. Idwal I6rch. M. Kadwaladyr vendigeit. M. [Fo. 38ᵃ] Katwalla6n. M. Kad6ga6n. M. Iago. M. Beli. M. Run hir. M. Maelg6n g6yned M. Kadwalla6n lla6hir. M. Einya6n yrth. M. Kuneda wledic.

[XXIII.]—𝔈inya6. a. Katwalla6n lla6hir. Deu vroder oedynt. Ac eu d6y vam oedynt chwioryd. Merchet y didlet brenhin g6ydyl fichti. ym pywys.

[XXIV.]—Rees gryc. M. Rees m6ynua6r. M. gruffud. M. Rees. M. te6d6r. M. Cadell. M. Einya6n. M. Ewein. M. Howel da. M. kadell. M. Rodri. ma6r.

[XXV.]—Rees gryc. M. Rees m6ynua6r. M. gwenlliant. brodyr y rees m6ynua6r. oedynt. maredud. a morgant. a maelg6n. meibon gwenlliant merch gruffud. M. Kynan.

[XXVI.]—Gruffud. M. Kynan. M. Iago. M. Idwal. M. Meuric. M. Itwal voel. M. Anara6t. Mab Rodri ma6r.

[XXVII.] [Fo. 38ᵇ]—Rees gryc mab merch mada6c. M. meredud. M. bledynt kynwyn. M. G6edylstan. M. kynvin. y kynvin h6n6. a gruffud vab llewelyn. a thrahayarn. M. Crada6c. tri broder oedynt. meibon y hagharat merch maredud mab. Ewein. M. howel da.

[XXVIII.]—Llywelyn. M. Iorwoerth. M. Ewein g6yned. M. gruffud. M. Cynan.

[XXIX.]—Llewelyn. M. marereda. Merch mada6c. M. maredud. bra6t oed varedud y rees gryc.

[XXX.]—Howel. M. Gron6y. M. Kad6ga6n. M. Elstan. M. Cuelyn. M. Cad6r. M. G6euneuuen. Merch Idnerth. M. Iorwoerth hirula6d.

[XXXI.]—Howel. M. Gron6y. M. Agharat merch La6r. mam hagharat oed leuku merch maredud. M. Ewein. M. Howel da.

[XXXII.] [Fo. 39ᵃ]—Howel. ac. Adam. a. phylib. a. thra-haearn. Iorwoerth. a. meilyr. gruffud. a chad6ga6n. a. ridyt. meibyon seissyll. M. llewelyn. M. Kad6ga6n. M. Elstan. a mam seissyl oed Ellel6.

[XXXIII.]—Ellel6 mam seissyll. M. llewelyn o vuellt. merch oed Ellel6 hono y Elidyr mab llywarch. M. bledri. M. mor mab. llowarch. M. G6ga6n keneu menrud a vu neidyr vl6ydyn am y von6gyl. y G6ga6n h6n6 a wnaeth aber G6yli.

ac yno y llad6yt ef a llewelyn. M. seissyll. tat gruffud. M. llewelyn.

[XXXIV.]—Keneu menrud oed h6n6. M. Pascen M. vrien reget. M. Kynuarch. M. meirchya6n. M. G6rguest. M. Keneu. M. Koel hen.

[XXXV.]—Rvn. M. Einya6n. M. Keneu. M. Coel hen. [XXXVI.]—Gwalla6c. M. llyenna6c. M. [Fo. 39b] Mar. M. Coyl hen.

[XXXVII.]—Morgant. M. Cleda6c. M. morgant mill. bra6t branud voel. M. dyuynwa6l. M. Carbonia6n. M. Coel hen.

[XXXVIII.]—Duna6t. M. pabo post prydein. M. Ceneu. M. Coel hen.

[XXXIX.]—Howel. M. Crada6c. M. meircha6n. M. Howel. M. Runya6n. M. Einya6n. M. Idwm. M. Cadwall. M. meic. M. Ewein. M. Cenlas. M. Ewein danwyn. M. Einya6n yrth. M. Cuneda Wledic.

[XL.]—Bleidut. M. Crada6c M. Iewana6l. M. Eiga6n. M. brorchuael. M. Eidan. M. Hoedle6. M. Podgen hen. M. Isaac. M. Einya6n. M. meuruc. M. dingat. M. eina6n. M. Duna6t. M. Cunada wledic.

[XLI.]—Kynan. M. Brochuael. M. einud. M. Brochuael. M. Sualda. M. ydris. M. Gweidno. M G6rent. vrabdruth. M. Katwaladyr. Katwaladyr a. chatwalla6n [Fo. 40a] deu vroder oedynt. meibon. Eueirya6n. M. tebia6n. M. Kuneda wledic.

[XLII.]—Howel da. M. Kadell. M. Rodri ma6r. M. meruyn vrych. Agharat oed mam Rodri. ma6r. merch veuruc. M. dyfynwal. M. Arden. M. Seissyll. M. Cleda6c. M. Aruodeu. M. Argloes. M. Pode6. M. Seruul. M. Vsai. M. Karedic. M. Kuneda wledic.

[XLIII.]—Dewi. M. sant. M. Ceredic. M. Cunada. wledic. [XLIV.]—Kynan buellt. M. Cedic tra6s. M. Ceredic. M. Kuneda wledic.

[XLV.]—Cenuur. M. Einyon. M. Keredic. M. Kuneda wledic. [XLVI.]—Amor M. morith. M. aidan. M. mor. M. Brochuael. M. Kuneda wledic. [XLVII.]—Gwynlli6. M. G6a6r. merch Keredic. M. Kynuelyn. M. meirya6n. M. Ceredic. M. Kun[ed]a wledic.

[XLVIII.]—G6ga6n. M. lla6r. M. Kedic. M. Keredic. M. Kuneda wledic. [XLIX.]—Bangar. M. Gardan. M. Karedic. M. dunun. M. An[fo. 40ᵇ]n6n. M. ceredic. M. Ceneu. M. Corun. M. Cunada wledic.

[L.]—[M]euruc. M. Elaed. M. Elud. M. Glas M. Elno M. docuael. M. Cuneda wledic.

Llyma enweu brenhined y brytanyeit.

[LI.]—Eneas ysc6ydwyn. Ascanius. Silnius. Brutus. Locrinus. Mada6c. Membyr. Efra6c. Brutus taryanlas. llyr lletieith. Bleidud. llyr. Cordiella. Cunada. Riwalla6n. G6rgan varyftr6ch. Seissyl. Iago. Kynvarch. Gorbannya6n. Porrex dyfynwa6l. Beli. G6rnet vrich hir. Cuelyn. Seissyll. Kynuarch. Dainus. Maredud. Gorbannia6n. Arthgal. Elidyr. Vigenius. Paredur. Gorbañya6n. M. Morgan. Einon. Idwal. Run. Cereint. Catellus. Coel. Porex. fferuex. ssulgen. Eldag . . Andre6. Kynon. Eliud. Cledno. Cloten. G6rgant. Meirya6n. Bledyn. Caap. Ewein. Seissyll. Blegywryt. Arth-[Fo. 41ᵃ]uael. Eidol. Reidon. Ryderch. Sam . . el. Pir. Cat6r. Eligullus. Beli. Ilud. Catwalla6n. Tenean. Kynuelyn. yn amser Kynuelyn. y ganet yn argl6yd ni iessu grist. Gwider. Marius. Coel. Lles. y lles h6n6 a anuones. att Eleutherius pab y adol6c danuon g6yr g6ybodus ar y ffyd gatholic y bregethu yr brytanyeit y ffyd mal y gellynt gaffel trugared raclla6. Ac ynteu a danuones d6an. a ffagan. Seuerus. Basian. Carancius. Alectus. Asclepiodotus. Coel. llyr. Constans. g6reic y constans h6n6 oed Elen. verch Coel. Constantinus. Constans. vanach. G6rtheyrn. Gwertheuyr vendigeit. Emrys wledic. Vthurpendreic. Arthur. Constantinus. Aurelius. Iuor. Maelg6n g6yned. Caterius. Catuan. Catwalla6n. Catwaladyr. vendigeit.

Note to Pedigrees.[1]

At the request of Dr. Isambard Owen, I have collated the foregoing pages of pedigrees with the original MS. I have carefully abstained from interfering with Mr. Phillimore's plan of reproduction. But I may say that capital black letters represent red Missal capitals in the MS., and that small black letters represent rubrics. Letters within brackets have been supplied by Mr. Phillimore; contractions have been extended and printed in *italics*. No attempt has been made to indicate characters touched by the pen of the rubricator, nor to reproduce all the special forms of letters in the original. The ll is in some instances ligatured and in some not, while in numerous cases it is difficult to decide whether it is, or is not, ligatured.

I have made a few corrections, and I suggest a few alternative readings.

Page 83, lines 9-10, " Marchara*irj*un." This is a most difficult word to read, especially in the case of the three letters *irj*. Possibly it may be read " Marchara*nh*un," but that is a guess, as is also the first reading; for both readings I am responsible.

Page 83, line 15, " Urgrgen." The second r is very doubtful, while the contraction mark over it makes it doubly so. But I cannot suggest any other letter, as the doubtful character is *not* like e.

Page 83, line 16, "hirblant ;" ? " hirblaut." Cf., page 88, line 20, where the reading is " hirula6t."

Page 84, lines 6-7, " Kembreith ;" ? " Keinvreith."

Page 84, line 8, " kyuor ;" ? " kynor." Cf. Llan-gynor.

Page 85, line 5, " Annueret ;" ? " Annueret."

---

[1] The above text was transcribed by the Editor, who has been prevented by illness from revising the proofs. Mr. J. Gwenogfryn Evans, the joint Editor of the *Old Welsh Texts*, kindly undertook the revision. [I. O., *Acting-Ed.*]

Page 86, line 6, " Pedur." I think there is no doubt about reading here " Peredur," for the usual mark of contraction is used.

Page 86, line 16, " bendigeit ;" ? " vendigeit."

Page 87, line 13, " tuclith ;" ? " luclith." See Prof. Rhŷs's *Welsh Lectures*, pp. 367 and 425.

Page 88, line 19, "G6euneuuen ;" ? " Gwenneuuen," or ·· Gwenuenuen." Cf. " Gwennwynwyn."

Page 89, line 14, " Idwm ;" ? " Idwin."

Page 90, line 20, " Eldag . ." The last letter or possibly two letters are quite illegible.

Page 90, line 23, " Sam .. el." This word is either Samuel or Samnel.

J. G. EVANS.

BONEDD Y SAINT*

FROM ABERYSTWYTH, NATIONAL LIBRARY OF WALES, MS. PENIARTH 12

This version of the *Bonedd y Saint* is believed to be different from any of those hitherto published, the most important of which appears to be the one called *Bonedd Saint Ynys Prydain,* printed in *Myv. Arch.,* ii, 23–5 (Gee's edition, p. 415), from a MS. in the Hafod Collection (probably since destroyed in the fire of 1807), collated with and (where defective) supplemented by a MS. called *Llyfr [John] Brook o Fawddwy,*[1] the age of which is not specified. This "Hafod" version is much longer than the one printed here, containing far more genealogies; the two documents are, however, not unlike, as far as the shorter one goes; up to which point both contain, for the most part, the same entries in a similar, though not identical, order. A copy of this "Hafod" version, presenting a few slight differences from the "Myvyrian" text (which seem mostly, if not entirely, traceable to the errors of one or both of the copyists), and made by Mr. Hugh Thomas early in the eighteenth century from a MS. stated to have been "wrote upon vellum about the year of our Lord 1250" and to have been "late in the custody of Mr. Edward Lhuyd of the Meuseum"(*sic*)—who died in 1709,— is found in the Harleian Collection of MSS., No. 4181, whence it has been reproduced in *Cambro-British Saints,* pp. 265–268,

---

[1] See *Myv. Arch.,* ii, 26 (Gee's ed., p. 417). Where is this MS. now, and who was John Brook of Mawddwy?

* Reprinted from *Y Cymmrodor* 7 (1886) 103–8, 133–4

with the inaccuracy so characteristic of that work.[1] It should be noted that the older MS. is said to have been *in the custody*, not *in the possession*, of E. Lluyd; hence it is possible that he was not the owner, but merely the borrower of it, and, if so, there is no difficulty in supposing that the MS. may have afterwards found its way into the Hafod Collection, and so have been identical with the Hafod MS. already mentioned.[2]

[1] See Rhys's *Lectures on Welsh Philology* (2nd ed., 1879), p. 425, and *Celtic Britain*, 1882, p. 288. Mr. Thomas's MS. has been annotated by some other person, who has inserted marginal notes mentioning various readings contained in MSS. of one "W. T." It is almost needless to say that in the *C.-B. S.* these notes have been bodily amalgamated with the text; and perhaps the most marvellous mistake occurs in one of these curious fusions on p. 267 (No. 37), where the words of the MS. *in Apogr.* [*i.e.* apographis] *penes W. T.* (= " in the copies belonging to W. T.") appear in the printed text as *in Yirgrpriws W. T.!* The fearful and wonderful word thus concocted would appear (if aught can be said to *appear*), from the somewhat chaotic context, to be the name of a district in Powys; and no doubt has, as such, duly exercised the patient research of members of the *Powys-Land Club.* For Hugh Thomas, see Jones's *Brecknockshire*, vol. i, p. 38, *note.*

[2] If, on the other hand, the MS. *belonged* to E. Lluyd, it cannot have been at Hafod in or before 1801, the date of the publication of the second volume of the *Myv. Arch.*, assuming the correctness of the statements made in *Eminent Welshmen*, p. 290, to the effect that Lluyd's collection was purchased in its entirety by Sir John Sebright, and that *his* collection was dispersed (for the first time) at the Sebright sale; it is also impossible (on the same assumptions) that any part of E. Lluyd's MSS. can have been destroyed (as is stated in *Cymmrodorion Transactions*, vol. i, p. 174, and in *Cambro-Briton*, ii, 201) in the Hafod fire, the date of which was March 13, 1807, seeing that the Sebright sale took place in April of that year. It is distinctly implied in *Eminent Welshmen*, p. 290, that all E. Lluyd's MSS. sold at the Sebright sale passed into the possession of Sir W. W. Wynn in 1807. This is quite incorrect. There are several volumes of E. Lluyd's at Peniarth (*Hengwrt MSS.*, Nos. 346–361) bought at the Sebright sale; a MS. now at the British Museum (*Addl. MSS..* No. 14,912) was also bought by Owain Myfyr at that sale; whilst MSS. of E. Lluyd's are to be found in the Bodleian Library (*Rawlinson MSS., B.* 467); and in the collec-

The other old copies of *Bonedd y Saint,* the existence of
which is known to the writer, are: (1) that contained in
Hengwrt MSS., No. 536, and written in about 1300; (2) the
Llanerch MS. (if that now exists), mentioned by Lewis
Morris in a letter to the Rev. Evan Evans (*Ieuan Brydydd
Hir*), dated July 4, 1760 (printed in *Cambrian Register,* i,
357–8), and also in the introduction to L. Morris's compilation called *Bonedd y Saint,* in *Myv. Arch.,* ii, 26 (Gee's
ed., p. 417); (3) the "Genealogies of Saints" in the *Llyfr
Llywelyn Offeiriad* (Jesus College, Oxon., MSS., No. 20),
a most valuable and probably unique text, quite distinct
from those represented by the Hafod MS. and Hengwrt
MS. No. 202, and relating mainly to South Wales,
especially to the family of Brychan Brycheiniog.[1]   A
copy of this is to be found in *Harl. MSS.,* No. 4181. The
oldest account of Brychan's family is that contained in
the short Latin tract *De sitv Brycheniavc,* occurring in a
MS. of the early 13th century (*Cottonian MSS., Vespasian
A.* xiv) in the British Museum. The Welsh forms and

tion of the Earl of Macclesfield (Shirburn MSS. 113. c. 18–21). A Welsh
Itinerary written by him was, in 1828, to be found in the collection of
Mr: John Mytton of Halston (*Cymmrodorion Trans.,* vol. ii, p. 46 ; 1828).
Most, if not all, of the Wynnstay portion of Edward Lluyd's MSS. were
burnt at the house of a bookbinder in London, together with the *White
Book of Hergest,* and other MSS.   As to this fire there is the following
MS. note by the late Miss Angharad Llwyd in her copy of *Cymmrodorion
Trans.,* vol. ii, p. 58: "In the conflagration caused by the burning of
Covent Garden Theatre in 1810, *the moiety* of the Sebright papers was
burnt: which were taken up to London by Mr. Ws. Wynn to be bound."
What is the explanation of "the moiety"?

[1] The writer is acquainted with (3), but not with (1) or (2). The
Llanerch MS., from its description in the *Myv. Arch.,* is clearly the
same as No. 2 of the MSS. at Llanerch in 1828, then belonging to the
Rev. G. Allanson, mentioned in the late Angharad Llwyd's "Catalogue
of Welsh MSS. in N. Wales" (*Cymmrodorion Trans.,* vol. ii, p. 46).   A
MS. note by her *ad locum* states that *No.* 1 of the list was "sold in 1857
for £9 by Mr. Dod", Mr. Allanson's successor at Llanerch.

glosses in that MS. show it to have been copied, by some one who did not understand Welsh, from an earlier MS. at least as old as the eleventh century ; it has been printed in *Cambro-British Saints*, pp. 272–5, with the greatest inaccuracy. A widely different version of this tract is to be found at the end of *Cott., Domitian*, I, where it bears the title of " Cognacio Brychan vnde brecheyniawc dict' est pars demetie .i. suthwallie". The writer was a Welshman (as is shown by his Welsh notes in other parts of the MS. volume), who wrote in about 1650 ; but the orthography of the Welsh names and words in his copy shows him to have taken it from a far earlier MS., probably of the thirteenth century.[1] A list of the descendants of Ceredig is appended to the end of this tract in *Vesp. A.* xiv, and other old genealogies of the Welsh Saints occur in their Latin and Welsh Lives (mostly published in *Cambro-British Saints*), *e.g.*, at the end of the Latin Life of St. Carannog, occurring in *Cott., Vesp. A.* xiv, and at the end of the Welsh Lives of St. David and St. Beuno, the oldest MS. of which (in *Hengwrt MSS.*, No. 57) dates from the thirteenth century.

Of the numerous texts of *Bonedd y Saint* which are known only from comparatively modern MSS., one occurs in *Harl. MSS.*, No. 4181, where it was copied by Mr. Hugh Thomas " from a MS. of Mr. John Lewis of Llwynweney,[2] in Rad-

---

[1] Appended to this copy is a transcript of parts of the other version, taken direct from *Vesp. A.* xiv, the orthography of which is retained. Is not this remarkable in a Welsh transcriber who lived at the period in question ? Theophilus Jones has printed the version from *Dom.* I. in his *Hist. of Breconshire*, vol. i, pp. 342–3, but he has failed to see that the words from " *Regressus*" to the end of the last paragraph in his printed text (which begin fo. 159ᵃ of the MS.) are merely an extract from the other version. (See *C.-B. Saints*, p. 273, ll. 7–12.)

[2] For him see *Arch. Camb.*, 4th Series, vol. i, pp. 75, 85–6, and *Camb. Reg.*, iii, 310–1. At *Arch. Camb.*, p. 75, he is said to be of *Llynwern ;* in the *C.-B. Saints* the place is spelt *Llynweny* at p. 269, and *Llanwenny* at

norshire, wrote about the time of Queen Elizabeth." It
has been printed in *Cambro-British Saints*, p. 269. Besides
the Llannerch MS., the *Llyfr Llywelyn Offeiriad,* and the
Llyfr John Brook o Fawddwy (already mentioned), several
MSS. containing versions of *Bonedd y Saint* are specified in
Myv. Arch., ii, 26 ; but none of these are there stated, or (it
is believed) otherwise known to be older than the sixteenth
century, except the *Llyfr Coch o Hergest*, the reference to
which must surely be a mistake, as no " Genealogies of Saints",
or documents containing them, are to be found in that MS.,
or have formed part of its contents for at least the last two
hundred years.[1] The various documents entitled *Achau y
Saint*, printed in the *Iolo MSS.* (pp. 100–146), are shown by
their form to be comparatively modern in their composition,
though no doubt they are based on older MSS.; the first two
were originally taken from the MSS. of Thomas ab Ifan of

p. 598, but in the preface to his *History of Great Britain* (London, 1729),
prefixed to the imperfect MS. of that work preserved in Harl. MS. 4872,
fos. 242, 245, it is spelt *Llynwene.* It seems to be the same as a place on
the banks of a tributary to the Edw river near Llanfihangel nant
melan, called in the Ordnance Map *Llanwenny,* by Jonathan Williams, in his *History of Radnorshire (Arch. Camb.*, 3rd Series, vol. iv,
p. 2) *Llewenny* and *Llanwen-nnau* (?) ; and by the author of *Llyfryddiaeth
y Cymry* (p. 354), " *Llynwenni* ger Maesyfed Newydd" (*i.e.*, " near New
Radnor", from which it is distant about five miles). Another *Llanwenny,*
three miles N.E. of Presteign, is in *Herefordshire.* Can any reader
of *Y Cymmrodor* inform the present writer where any account of this
Mr. John Lewis is to be found? He was the owner of MSS. Nos. 228,
269, 270, and 271 in the Hengwrt collection : in the first of these he is
described by his friend and contemporary, Dr. John Dafydd Rhys, as
of *Kinarsley* (? Kinnersley in Herefordshire) ; and it is suggested in
Arch. Camb., loc. cit., that he was the same as one John Lewis of
Harpton. He was a barrister, and lived in the reigns of Elizabeth and
James I. In *Llyfryddiaeth y Cymry*, p. 354, he is unaccountably confused with John Lewis of Manarnawan, Pembrokeshire, who lived 50
or 100 years later, and for whom see Fenton's *Pembrokeshire*, pp. 4–7.

[1] See the catalogue of its contents in *The Cambro-Briton*, vol. ii, pp.
75, 106.

Tre Brynn in Llangrallo (*Anglicè* Coychurch), Glamorgan-shire, by whom the first was written in about 1670. Much valuable local information is, however, contained in these genealogies.

Boned y seint.

DE6i ap sant ap keredic ap kuneda wledic.   A non verch
gẏnẏr o gaer ga6c ẏmẏnẏ6 ẏ6 ẏ vam.

Doguael ap ith*ael* ap keredic ap kuneda wledic.

Caranawc ap korun ap keredic ap kuneda wledic.

Tẏsilia6 ap enoc ap etwin ap keredic ap kuneda wledic.

Kẏnnelẏn ap bleidud ap meiria6n ap tẏbrani ap keredic ap
kuneda wledic.

Edern ap beli ap run ap maelg6n g6ẏned ap katwalla6n
lla6ir ap einion ẏrth ap kuneda wledic.

Einion[1] vrenhin ẏn lleẏn. a seirioel ẏmpenmon : a meirion
ẏmeirionẏd.   A meirion ẏn ẏ kantref.   Meibion ẏ6ein danwẏn
ap Einion[1] ẏrth ap kuneda wledic.   katwaladẏr vendigeit ap
katwalla6n ap katwan ap iago ap beli ap run ap maelg6n
g6ẏned ap einion wwr ap pabo post prẏdein.   A dwẏuei
(Col. 2) verch leinia6c ẏ vam.   assa ap sawẏl benuchel ap
priabo post prẏdein.   A gwenassed verch rein hael ẏ vam.

Kẏndeẏrn garthwẏs ap ẏwein ap vrẏen.   A dẏfuẏr verch
leidun llẏda6 ẏ vam o dinas etwin ẏn ẏ gogled.

Gwrwst letl6m ap g6eith bangaer ap elphin ap vrẏen reget.
A chreir6ẏ verch glẏtno eidin ẏ vam.

Cadell ap vrẏen buan ap ẏsg6ẏn ap llẏwarch hen.   lleudat
a maglan o goet alun.   Ac eleri o bennant gwẏtherin ẏn
rẏuonẏoc.   A thetk6ẏn.   A thẏurẏdawt ẏg keredigion is koet
meibion dingat ap nud hael ab seinill ap kedic ap dẏuẏnwal.
A thenoi verch leidun llẏdaw eu mam.

Padern ap petrun ap ẏmerllẏda6.

Trunẏo ap diuangi ap ẏmerllẏda6.

Terillo a thẏgei meibion Ithael hael o lẏda6.   A llechit ẏn
arllechwed eu chwaer.

_____
[1] Apparently altered from *Ennon*. The old form was "Enniaun".

Kẏbi ap selẏf ap gereint ap erbin ap custennin goreu.

Padric ap morud ap goron6. o waredoc ẏn aruon ẏ vam.

Iẏstin ap gereint brawt kustennin.

Tathwrch ẏn abererch ẏn lleẏn. A thang[6n] ẏn llangoet
ẏmon. A maethlu ẏg kaerdega6c ẏmon. meibion karada6c
vreichwras ap llẏr marini.

Beuno gassulsẏch [ap] bengi ap gwẏnlli6 ap gli[6ẏs] ab tegit
ap kadell. A phe[ren] [Fo. xxv[b]] verch leidun llẏda6 ẏ vam.

Cannen a g6ẏnlli6 ap gli6is ap tegit ap kadell : o llan gathus
o went.

Tẏssilia6 ap brochuael ẏsgithra6c ap kẏngen ap kadell.
o ardun verch babo post prẏdein ẏ vam.

Llẏwelẏn ẏn ẏ trallwng ap tẏgonwẏ ap teon ap g6ineu
deuureud6ẏt. A g6rnerth ap lle6elẏn. elhaearn ẏmaes
kegitua. ẏmpo6ẏs. A llwch elhaearn ẏg kedewein. A chẏn-
haearn ẏn ẏnẏs gẏnhaearn ẏn eidonẏd. Meibion eharnuael
ap kẏndr6ẏn.

Peblic sant ap maxen wledic. Ac elen verch eudaf ap
karada6c ẏ vam.

Peris sant kardinal o ruuein.

TEXTS

GOSPEL-BOOKS

It was early the practice to write down sworn information on the pages of monastic illuminated Gospel-texts, thereby enhancing the binding force of the oath. More extensive texts of moment to the monastery were strengthened by inclusion within the same binding as the Gospels. The earliest such entries are those in the *Book of Teilo* (Chad) (unpublished), a manuscript in Lichfield Cathedral, including the memoranda and a selection of other signatures reproduced in facsimile, with transcription and translation in *LL*, beginning *c.* 800, with the statement that Gelhi bought the Gospel-book for a 'best horse' and presented it to the monastery. The *Book of Armagh* (diplomatic edition, ed. John Gwynn, 1913; facsimile of Patrician entries, ed. E. J. Gwynn, 1937; Patrician material, Stokes, *VT*, etc.), written *c.* 807, binds up the lives and traditions of Patrick with a few grant-memoranda and a very large quantity of assertions of entitlement to Church-lands, in front of the New Testament text.

The *Bodmin Gospels* (now British Library MS. Add. 9381, unpublished), of the early tenth century, contains a large number of records of manumissions, Cornish and English, whose earliest date is 941 (transcribed Stokes, *RC*, 1, 180-2, 332: Förster, in *Grammatical Miscellany . . . Otto Jespersen*, Copenhagen, 1930, 77). The *Book of Llandaff* (quasi-diplomatic edition, *Liber Landavensis*, ed. J. G. Evans, 1893, replacing W. J. Rees, Llandovery, 1840) is a twelfth-century copy of a Gospel-book on the Armagh model, retaining only the Gospel of Matthew, with the Lives of the monastery's principal saints and a very large quantity of memoranda of grants held to have been made all over south Wales from the late sixth century onward, their wording doctored to transform them into grants to Llandaff. A copy of the similar *Book of Llancarfan* reproduces only the Life of Cadoc, with the grant-memoranda, and is published as *Vita Cadoci* in *VSB*, 24-140. The *Books of Durrow, Lindisfarne and Kells* (facsimiles) contain a few marginalia, concerned with their own composition (Durrow and Lindisfarne; *cf.* **E**, Patrick, Aediluald) and with late grant-memoranda (Kells). Many Continental Irish Gospel-books and other manuscripts contain a variety of glosses and marginalia.

HONORIUS'S LETTER

(John Morris's MSS. contained very little of this section which has therefore been written by Mr Stephen Johnson. It thus represents his own views, which do differ, in emphasis at least, from those contained in *The Age of Arthur*. The reader is, however, presented with the text, a translation and notes. – *Ed.*)

Zosimus vi, 10, 2: Ὀνωρίου δὲ γράμμασι πρὸς τὰς ἐν βρεττανίᾳ χρησαμένου πόλεις φυλάττεσθαι παραγγέλλουσι

Gothofredus conjectured, in his great commentary on the Theodosian Code (vol. iv, p. 212), ἐν βρουτίᾳ instead of ἐν βρεττανίᾳ

'After Honorius had written letters to the cities of Britain, recommending them to look after their own defence, and after he paid off his troops with the money which Heraclian had sent, Honorius relaxed completely, since he had gained the favour of his troops everywhere.'

Notes

(a) The Text
The spelling βρεττανίᾳ is normal in the texts of Zosimus for 'Britain'. In his edition of the Theodosian Code, however, Gothofredus suggested the emendation 'Bruttium' for Britain at this point, arguing from the context that affairs in Britain were irrelevant at this precise moment. He pointed out that according to Zosimus's own context, Britain was technically in revolt from the Emperor (ever since the appointment of her own Emperor Marcus, in 406), and there was no reason why Honorius should concern himself with such far-off affairs now. More in context would be Honorius's concern about Bruttium, an area now directly threatened by the advance of Alaric, mentioned by Zosimus in the previous chapter.

The emendation is no more, however, than a conjecture, and none of the manuscripts retains a variant reading which might support this alteration to the text. Indeed, general principles of textual criticism, in that mention of Britain at this point is to some extent a *lectio difficilior*, suggest strongly that it would be wrong to alter it here.

(b) The Immediate Context
This aspect was discussed most fully by E. A. Thompson in *Britannia*, 8 (1977), 315-6. The sentence in which Honorius's letter to the cities of Britain is mentioned sits

78

within the narrative of Alaric's siege of Rome in 409 and his assault thereafter on Bologna and the cities of Liguria (hence the conjecture 'Bruttium' above). The date is thus A.D. 410, and probably early in the year.

The sentence itself falls into two parts: the first half is a genitive-absolute clause in which Honorius is named, as if the main clause of the sentence was not going to have Honorius as the subject. The main clause, surprisingly, does carry Honorius's name (this time in the nominative) as the main subject of the sentence. An attempt has been made in the translation above to preserve this awkwardness. Zosimus clearly changed his mind mid-sentence about what he intended to say; thus any indication of the original context cannot really be gleaned.

(c) The Interpretation
Although these eleven brief words of Zosimus may not be considered adequate witness for every hypothesis which has been built upon them, certain points are worth making and are of some significance.

In the first place, the Greek phrase does not allow us to know whether Honorius wrote one or several letters. Thus the Emperor may have written a separate letter to each of the cities of Britain or a single letter to some form of provincial council. The idea that there was still a provincial council with which Honorius in this instance corresponded is common to many of the writers and commentators on the period.

The main difficulties are provided by the general context within Zosimus's narrative of the history which he is telling. In 406-7, we are told, the British troops set up a British emperor, Marcus. For some reason, he and his successor proved inadequate for the emergency which occurred at the very end of 407, a disastrous raid into Gaul across the Rhine by barbarian tribes. Since this threatened to cut Britain off from all contact with Rome and mainland Europe (thereby depriving the British troops of any chance of being paid for their services), the third British emperor appointed by the troops there was a soldier, Constantine by name, who lost no time in raising a force and shipping it across to Gaul. Once there, he spent some time in repairing the Rhine-defences but made no apparent attempt to harry the raiders back across the river. Constantine's force seems relatively easily to have become dispersed, and was split up between southern Gaul and Spain. In the meantime, there was a barbarian raid on Britain. Although Zosimus does not give a full version of what happened, for he suggests that the barbarians were the same Vandals who had crossed the Rhine and had turned southwards through Gaul, it was probably of quite serious proportions. The crucial passage here is Zosimus vi, 5, 2, in which 'The barbarians (from beyond the Rhine) overran everything at will and reduced the inhabitants of the British island and some of the people of Gaul to the necessity of rebelling from the Roman empire and living by themselves, no longer obeying the Romans' laws. The Britons, therefore, taking up arms and fighting on their own behalf, freed the cities from the barbarians who were pressing upon them.' (Translation by E. A. Thompson.)

It is not our concern here to elucidate the exact nature of these events, nor further to discuss the type of rebellion which seems to be implied, but merely to note first the rejection of Roman laws (and hence by inference those who had maintained the Roman order), and, second, the spontaneous freeing of the cities from the barbarian threat. This view provides an adequate context for Honorius's letter in the first place by eliminating all the Roman officials (*duces, comites*, or even the *uicarius* himself) to whom such a missive might normally have been sent. Also, it identifies the cities, now freed from their surrounding barbarians (presumably the Saxons, for there is an independent testimony of a raid by them), as the centres of power. Whether such power was wielded separately or as a joint council of cities, following in some way the provincial council, is a matter for speculation. Thus Zosimus's account of the letter of Honorius sent to the cities of Britain is in no way inconsistent with anything which he had written previously about Britain.

There are still difficulties, however, which make one suspect that there were elements of the story which Zosimus had failed to reveal. Technically, Britain had been in revolt from the Roman empire from the moment when her troops appointed Marcus as emperor in 406. This would have been the natural time for Britain to expel any of the 'Roman' officials who wished to leave and not to become associated with an officially unrecognised regime. In all probability, therefore, there was a lack of top Roman administration within the province from 406 onwards. Yet Zosimus puts the rejection of Roman laws in 408. One might rightly judge that the appointment of a usurping emperor does not necessarily mean a rejection of Roman law and order – indeed, it might often signify tighter control over a weakened administration. It is hard, therefore, to interpret what Zosimus saw as having happened in 408.

The existence of the 'provincial council' also needs some scrutiny. For several of the provinces of the Roman world there is evidence that from a proportion of the most eminent decurions a council of this nature was formed. Whether this had to have representatives from all *ciuitates*, how often it met, and any assessment of the sorts of business which came before it are all unclear. In common with many of the constitutional forms of the later Roman world, much of its business may have been normal declamatory statements of loyalty to the emperor and the *uicarius*, and the council may have been called upon to meet only once a year, on the imperial anniversary. Although the rather functional and depressing eulogy of the Emperor and his administration may have been the main order of such meetings, there is evidence that in some cases genuine grievances were aired, more by persistence than by rational argument: the evidence for this comes from records of similar late imperial meetings and councils held in eastern provinces, where the records have happened to survive. The council, however, is unlikely to have assumed anything approaching a parliamentary or policy-making function. On the face of it, such a body – even supposing that it was to be found at all within later Roman Britain (there is no independent evidence) – seems an unlikely vehicle to have stepped immediately into a vacuum left by the breakdown of imperial Roman control.

We are now in a position to tackle the main problem, that of Honorius's letter itself. It is generally agreed that the letter (or letters) is a reply – a rescript – to some enquiry from the cities of Britain. Was it the provincial council which wrote? And if so, what was the query or request?

Ostensibly, any British city or council ought not to have been in contact with Honorius at all. Britain was technically in revolt from Rome since the establishment of her own emperor. Technically, therefore, contact with Honorius was treason to the British emperor, Constantine III. It has thus been surmised that there were rival political factions involved: broadly, those who supported the idea of an independent Britain and those who wished to see a return to legitimate 'Roman' government. Clearly, whatever interpretation one puts on the request to Honorius, it is no more than speculation, partly in the light of what may be only a half-told story by Zosimus, and partly in the light of modern assessment of the political motives and pressures of the parties involved. As has been shown above, we are not at all clear exactly who sent the initial enquiry, and this makes the task of deduction the more difficult.

The initial letter from Britain to Honorius has perhaps most often been seen as an appeal for help. As Thompson rightly remarked, however, there was no imminent danger against which the cities needed defending at this moment, since the barbarian raid, according to Zosimus's own narrative, had been roundly beaten off. Thompson went on to suggest that the threat from which the British cities needed protection was not the barbarians themselves, but the *Bacaudae* – a sort of peasant *maquis* – who by his own account of the events of 408 had already assisted the cities to free themselves from the barbarian menace, and who had now turned upon these centres of Roman power, traditionally the target of their form of disaffection. C. E. Stevens suggested that the British cities wrote to Honorius to justify their having taken up arms against the barbarians. Technically, the bearing of arms by a civilian was an offence under Roman laws, but it is hard to see why such fine points of legal detail as this should be of any concern to the cities of Britain at the time, nor is it clear why this, of all matters, should have been raised with Honorius at the time.

Thompson's suggestion that the appeal for help was for assistance against the *Bacaudae* is awkward, too. If we suppose that the revolt of 408 was a Bacaudic one, it is difficult to see a consistent motive for these bands of peasant militia: if assault on the cities had always been their aim, one might have expected the *Bacaudae* to join the barbarians in carrying this out, rather than apparently going to the trouble of freeing the cities from this problem, and then deciding to continue the assault on their own. It would make better sense to see the *Bacaudae* as sufferers during the barbarian raids, and turning their attention, after the raid had been beaten off, to retribution against the cities, which had emerged unscathed from the barbarian attacks. Reading the relevant passages of Zosimus, however, fails to support such an elaborate set of hypotheses. In fact, to assume that the letter to Honorius was requesting assistance leads to all sorts of difficulties which go far beyond Zosimus's text.

Any fresh interpretation of this deduced letter to Honorius has to answer and satisfy as many of these criticisms as possible. It has to explain why a request or a letter should be sent to Honorius rather than to Constantine. It has to guess at the context for such a letter, as also its content. It is always difficult to guess what the question might have been to any given answer – we do not even know that the letter to Honorius was a question or request; it might easily have been a statement, to which Honorius's reply was an official acknowledgement only. What needs to be explained in this case is why a relatively routine matter like this should find its way onto the pages of Zosimus as one of the more important asides meriting inclusion within his imperial history. Did Zosimus see a copy of this letter? Or did he pick out from some other source (where?) the gist which he considered later to be most important? And how can we be certain that any letter which Honorius or his imperial administration wrote was in fact a relevant or sensible reply to whatever had been posed?

No approach to Honorius at this time from Britain can have been either a direct appeal for help or a discussion of the 'finer points of *Lex Julia de vi publica*'. All that the provincial council could do – and a singularly fitting task for that particular body – was to declare in no uncertain terms their loyalty to the Emperor. Within the political climate of Britain of the day, this may have been a particularly contentious thing to do, depending on what Zosimus and we understand by the fact that the Britons were no longer living according to the Roman laws. But Britain was in fairly desperate straits: Constantine had taken away a large part of its army, sorely depleted as it had been over the last decades by constant withdrawals. The cities of Britain had weathered one barbarian storm, but there was no guarantee that they could do it again. The remaining authorities needed leaders for such troops as were left to garrison the island, money to pay them, and tighter control from Rome. All these could be provided only by the legitimate emperor.

What better way, then, to invite imperial intervention within Britain again than to write declaring complete loyalty to the Emperor, and to catalogue the events of 407-9 showing how desperate was the need of an effective military presence within Britain. It is not difficult to see how such a letter would come to be drafted, probably at an emergency meeting of the provincial council. It would include a brave account of the way in which the Britons had already had to defend themselves. We can also imagine how Honorius, besieged in Italy by Alaric and unable to spare any of his troops or his crack generals to strengthen the defences of part of the Roman world so far from his own concerns in Italy, would have taken the request. Honorius was completely unable to assist: if the British cities expected his intervention, they must have been bitterly disappointed. It may be, however, that their declaration of loyalty was nicely timed to come at a moment when it would be gratefully accepted: the practical implications insofar as renewed military occupation of Britain were concerned would be studiously ignored.

What, then, of Honorius's reply? In the light of this discussion, it is probable that his 'instruction' to look after their own defence was not a startling order at all. It came merely as the endorsement of a course of action that the British cities had already undertaken. Faced with a decision on matters where it could neither intervene nor enforce its authority, Honorius's administration fell back on what was no more than a temporising reply – an endorsement of the Britons' actions and a tacit recognition that, for the moment, the Roman military was unable to help. In all probability, no one intended this to be the last involvement of Rome with her British provinces, but so, in the event, it turned out. The letter of Honorius may thus have been taken to have far more historical significance by Zosimus and more modern historians than perhaps it deserves. In reality, it could be seen as a classic case of a powerless bureaucratic administration being presented with a problem which provided within its own elements the germ of what they saw as its own solution. For Honorius, the endorsement of the British cities' actions and the acceptance of their protestations of loyalty was at once inexpensive and magnanimous, and in no way prejudiced any further Roman involvement with Britain. It may not, however, have been the answer which the British cities had hoped to elicit.

LAWS

The principal comprehensive collections are *The Ancient Laws and Institutes of Wales*, ed. Aneurin Owen, 1841, and *of Ireland* (Brehon Laws), ed. W. N. Hancock, *et al.*, 6 vols, 1865-1901 (with translations); Felix Liebermann, *Die Gesetze der Angelsachsen*, 1898-1916 – superseding Schmid (1858) and Thorpe (1865) – and a useful reprint of most of the main texts with translations in F. L. Attenborough, *The Laws of the Earliest English Kings*, 1922. The earliest Scottish laws (*Acts of Parliament of Scotland*, Vol. 1) are later medieval and are so complex a mixture of developed Irish, British, English, Scandinavian and Norman practice that they offer very little information relevant to the seventh century or earlier. The Continental Germanic laws, however, mostly of the ninth and tenth centuries, have some bearing on English and Welsh law; the most relevant are the *Lex Saxonum* and the *Lex Anglorum et Werinorum, hoc est Thuringorum*. The edition of C. von Schwerin, in the small *MGH* series (*Fontes Iuris Germanici Antiqui*, 1918) contains both, with references to the corresponding passages in all known Germanic laws given for each separate clause.

The only comprehensive survey of the whole of these laws, of the British Isles and of Germanic Europe, is that of F. Seebohm, *Tribal Custom in Anglo-Saxon Law*, 1911; *cf. The Tribal System in Wales*, 1904, and *The English Village Community*, 1883.

The Germanic and English laws tersely rule on a limited range of topics, principally the compensations due to king and Church and to individuals resulting from the violation of the person and/or rights, and presuppose the existence of a customary law which has not been preserved. They are, however, either the original texts of the law pronounced by the kings named, or very close to them: the earliest are those attributed to Aethelbert (died 616), to Hlothere, Eadric (*c.* 680) and Wihtred (6 September 695) of Kent, and to Ine of Wessex (*c.* 690).

The Welsh and Irish laws are much bulkier, the main printed collections containing about 1,000 pages of text, and cover a much wider range of stages of interpreting the meaning by commentary and comparison of relevant texts, for the obscurity of word and construction masks many problems until translation into a living language grapples with them.

The difficulty with the Welsh laws is to decide how much is due to Edward I, how much to Hywel Dda, and how much to ancient custom which he set down and codified. There are some fixed points. The earliest post-Roman coins found in Wales are those of Alfred (died 899), and therefore values expressed in money cannot be significantly earlier than Hywel's time. An extensive section giving the prices of damage to various parts of the body in minute detail (*VC* 2, 23; *DC* 2, 17; *GC* 2, 6-7; *ALW* 2, 15; 2, 21) reproduces, with minor variations, groups of rulings common to most Germanic Continental codes (*Lex Saxonum*, 4-7, 11-13; *Lex Anglorum*, 8-24; *cf.* references there given to other Germanic codes), and in two English codes

(*Aethelbert*, 33-72; *Alfred*, 44-77). The variants are closest to the West Saxon version: the prices equate the Irish valuation (3 cows = 1 *cumal* = 1 oz silver), the Welsh (3 cows = 1 [oz] silver), and the English (1 cow = 20-24 pence = originally 1 shilling), since the value of a full-grown two-year-old cow is 20-24 pence (*GC* 2, 11 1), and the worth (*Guerth;* cf. West Saxon *wer*) of a freeman is 'three score (and three)' cattle, the equivalent of 1,200/1,300 pence, close to the freeman's worth in Alfred's Wessex, 1,000 pence, 200s. The preceding section in most codes gives prices in pence for 250 tools, weapons, garments, furnishings and commodities, and both sections look like a deliberate attempt to adapt the Welsh economy to a monetary system and to trade with the English, almost certainly the work of Hywel, and certainly not the work of Edward I, by whose times English values had changed considerably. The section is also considerably valuable for English custom and English economy. The injuries named are selected from their Germanic originals: penalties for pulling a man's hair are found only in the English versions, and among the Saxons, Frisians, custom and enactment.

The Welsh texts consist of half-a-dozen recensions, of varying dates and regions, of a code attributed to Hywel Dda (died 950). One of the extant manuscripts was brought to Edward I, who made some changes, after the English conquest in the late thirteenth century.

Many of the Irish texts are works of jurisprudence rather than of legislation, treatises of different dates, on varying scales, and are supplemented by a number of ecclesiastical canons and penitentials (Kenney, 235 ff.), including the *Collectio Canonum Hibernensis* (Kenney, 247; H. Wasserschleben, *Die irische Kanonensammlung,* ed. 2, 1885), which is a manual of contradictory precedents to be used at the discretion of judges, published *c.* 700 × 725. It concerns British and English as well as Irish law since many of the manuscripts are Breton, and its principal authorities, apart from the Scriptures, the Fathers and the synods, are Patrick, Gildas, Finnian (of Moville?), Adomnán of Iona and Theodore of Canterbury, the last two very recently dead when it was written. Substantial sections of Irish secular law, in particular those contained in the *Senchus Mór* and *Bretha Nemed* tracts, including the 'Small Primer' (*Uraicecht Becc*), adapt originals in Old Irish (extreme date-limits *c.* 700 × 950, Jackson, *LHEB* 7) and were dated by MacNeill (*PRIA* 36 C, 1923, 255 and *Celtic Ireland*, 96 ff., with commentary on the 'Small Primer'), and by D. A. Binchy (*Ériu* 18, 1958, 44) to 'the eighth century or earlier', some possibly composed about 680. Many texts are, however, of uncertain date, and many are not contained in the main collections. Discussions, particularly of Irish texts, are therefore frequently constrained to cite directly from unpublished manuscripts, or from those published only in facsimile or without translation; or to clarify the mistakes of the main printed collections. Since verbal exactitude matters more for legal texts than most, effort cannot avoid concentrating on the first stage of establishing exactly which words were written when.

The Saxons price fingers both according to which finger is damaged, and to which finger-joints; Alfred prices the fingers but not the joints; the Welsh the joints but not the fingers; Alfred and the Welsh price the tongue, the Continental Germans do not. These and other variants, with the considerable differences in the relative values placed on different injuries, concern the kind of violence anticipated in each society, and also date back to a common original from which all versions select. The extensive section on prices is not reproduced in any English or Germanic text. It is, however, an attempt to price the commodities named in English currency, and is therefore relevant to the English economy.

On the other hand, many sections seem earlier. The sections on the royal household of the king of all Wales cannot be earlier than Hywel, or possibly Rhodri, died 877; but they adapt to the supreme king the practices and charges claimed by regional kings in the past. Parts of the administrative terminology and organisation are also traceable in areas of northern Britain which passed from British political control at the end of the sixth century and should therefore have originated no later. The hereditary freedom of the *boneddig* subsisted among the Welsh of the seventh century. Some of the institutions of Welsh law are also found in the charters of Brittany and should therefore be at least as old as the sixth century. Much of the law concerning the family, marriage, divorce, and inheritance is so close to the corresponding Irish customary law, so alien to Germanic, Roman or ecclesiastical law, that it strongly suggests a common origin not later than the Roman conquest of Wales in the late first century A.D., while other important developments in the organisation of the very large kinship-group suggest rather an origin in the eighth or ninth century. The stratification of the laws is, however, not likely to be sorted out with confidence until a systematic comparison becomes possible between the corresponding clauses in the different versions, illustrated by relevant evidence from Irish, English and Germanic practice.

Modern studies of some of the wider aspects of the bearing of the laws on social history include: Karl Brunner, *Deutsche Rechstgeschichte*, 1906; H. M. Chadwick, *Studies in Anglo-Saxon Institutions*, 1905, and *The Origin of the English Nation*, 1907, rev. 1924; J. Braude, *Die Familiengemeinschaften der Angelsachsen*, 1932, as well as the work of Pollock, Maitland, Vinogradoff and others, and a considerable number of specialised studies, the scattered writings of Eoin MacNeill, especially his kindly but decisive demolition of the misconceptions of P. W. Joyce, *Social History of Ancient Ireland*, 1903, still sometimes cited and often assumed (cf. particularly MacNeill, *Celtic Ireland*, 1921 [lectures delivered 1905-7], pp.152 ff.), and R. Thurneysen and others, *Studies in Early Irish Law*, 1936, concerned with the status of women, marriage, inheritance, etc. Evidence on the kind of questions illustrated by the laws in other lands was discussed by W. F. Skene, *Celtic Scotland*, 1876-80, based on the material assembled in his *Chronicles of the Picts and Scots*, 1867, which has not yet been superseded by more recent work on a comparable scale. Some work has been done on the supporting documentation, notably D. Whitelock, *Anglo-Saxon Wills*, 1930; but the English, Welsh and Irish grants and charters still await a critical edition.

MARTYROLOGIES

Notably of *Tallaght*, ed. Best and Lawlor, London, 1931; of *Donegal*, ed. Todd and Reeves (trans. O'Donovan), Dublin, 1864; of *Oengus* the Culdee, ed. and trans. Stokes, London, 1905 (commonly described as the *Félire of Oengus*; of *Gorman*, ed. and trans. Stokes, London, 1895. These documents are all described as *Félire* (Calendar) in Irish, Martyrology in English. There is no obvious rational reason for the modern habit of quoting the word *Félire* in English texts for Oengus but not his fellows. The main information offered by these texts is the district where the saint worked and the district where he was born, which usually agree with the main sources; and the saint's pedigree, which often disagrees and is by any comparative evidence impossible, although it may incorporate parts of normal pedigrees of the area concerned. They often locate obscure individuals otherwise known only from a single casual reference; and they sometimes give anecdotes about individuals. They were discussed by Grosjean, *AB*, 51, 1933, 117 ff.

MUIRCHÚ'S LIFE OF ST PATRICK

INTRODUCTION

Patrick was the effective founder of the Christian Church in Ireland. He was consecrated bishop and came to Ireland in 432. He stayed in Ireland until his death, about 30 years later, and was the first Christian to make any substantial number of converts, and to leave behind him a lasting organised church.

His life and work are exceptionally well recorded.[1] Two of his own writings are preserved; they are the only documents that have survived from the British Isles in the century after the fall of Rome; and a biography, composed by a Leinster priest named Muirchu about 200 years later, drew upon lost contemporary texts. These documents are here reproduced, in the original Latin, with an English translation.

But in spite of unusually full and clear evidence, the story of Patrick has suffered feverish distortion at the hands of interested ecclesiastics, from the later seventh century onwards. He founded and organised a church, with many converts, including several persons of royal and princely origin in north eastern Ireland. But though converts were many, they were still a small minority, and Christianity did not in his time become the national faith of the Irish. In the words of the modern scholar most deeply acquainted with the literature of early Christian Ireland, Patrick 'was not entirely forgotten, but such evidence as we have regarding the two hundred years following his death seems to show that his memory had slipped into the background of old and far-off things.'[2]

The traditions of Ireland and Britain emphasise that in southern and central Ireland the Christian church was founded independently of Patrick, a generation after his time, and also long remained a minority faith. The mass of the Irish population was not converted until the expansion of the monastic reform, in the middle decades of the sixth century. A hundred years thereafter, the Irish church was torn by controversy between those who sought conformity with Rome and Europe in organisation and in external symbols and those who clung to traditional ways. Controversy was fierce for more than two generations, and in its later stages the adherents of conformity with Rome revived and magnified the name of Patrick, the true founder of the Irish Church, who had been canonically ordained and had conformed with Rome. The zealous interest preserved his own writings and Muirchu's biography, but it also submerged his memory in a flood of added fiction.

The only valid evidence for Patrick's life is contained in his own writings, in Muirchu's biography, and in the external records that explain the circumstances of his appointment. He himself describes his background and youth. He was a Roman Briton. His father was a *decurion*, a town councillor and local magnate, and also a Christian deacon; his grandfather, and perhaps also his great-grandfather, had been a Christian priest. His father owned a substantial estate, maintained by a large number of servile cultivators, probably in southwestern Britain. At the age of 16 he was taken prisoner by Irish raiders, and served as a slave herdsman for six years, probably in north-eastern Ireland, until he escaped. He travelled 200 miles to find a ship, and after three days' voyage landed in a deserted countryside, which he and the ships' crew traversed for 28 days before they came to human habitation. The long voyage suggests a landfall in Gaul rather than in Britain, and the extensive uninhabited land suggests Brittany. The ship that carried him in his clandestine escape was evidently no ordinary merchant, but was manned by emigrants or refugees, for the captain and crew abandoned it on making land, and Patrick says nothing of storm or shipwreck.

Patrick also says nothing of the next few years, save that at some time he acquired friends in Gaul; but Muirchu reports that he spent a long time at Auxerre; and one fragment, perhaps from Patrick's pen, also reports a visit to 'the islands of the Tyrrhene sea'[3] as well as to Italy. These were chief centres of the reform movement that was reshaping western Christianity in Patrick's youth. Until the end of the 4th century, Christianity had been almost entirely a religion of the towns, so much so that the Latin word for countryman, *paganus*, became the ordinary word for heathen or non-Christian; and the great majority of bishops were urbane, well-to-do gentlemen, with little sympathy for the rustic boor, and no interest at all in the baptism of barbarians beyond the frontier.

Established views were challenged and shaken by Martin of Tours, a generation before Patrick's time. He was the first hermit in Europe. In the east, holy ascetics of the desert were older than Christianity, and in the early 4th century Christian ascetics flocked to the deserts of Egypt and the Near East in large numbers. They were termed *monachi*, monks (from the Greek word *monos*, lone) because each sought to live alone by himself in direct communion with God; but they were so numerous that they were compelled to live in large communities, the first Christian monasteries. In the west, a few wealthy individuals took a personal monastic vow, and lived retired ascetic lives on their own estates with a few companions. From the later 4th century, some reforming bishops encouraged their diocesan clergy to take personal monastic vows, and housed them in monasteries attached to their cathedrals.

Martin quickly earned widespread fame and honour as the only solitary ascetic of Europe, and against his will was chosen bishop of Tours in 372. He refused to live in the bishop's town house, and established himself in a cave two miles from the city, where he established a monastery and a school for 80 monks. He offended his fellow bishops because he was 'shabby and ill dressed'[4] and no gentleman; and he was also the first to preach systematically to country people in his diocese. His two best known pupils were Victricius, who became bishop of Rouen, and is the first Latin Christian known to have made converts and founded monasteries among barbarians beyond the frontiers, in the territory that is now Belgium, and Amator, who became bishop of Auxerre, and there founded a cathedral monastery.

Martin died in 397. Just before his death, Victricius visited Britain, and won decisive majority support for Martin's reforms in a synod of British bishops; probable immediate consequences of his visit included the foundation of monasteries at St. Albans and at Whithorn in Galloway, among the barbarians, and of a church of Martin at Canterbury. But Martin's initiative was not widely followed in Europe. Reform took a new direction after 410, when the capture of Rome by the Goths shocked many men into new thinking. A young nobleman named Honoratus founded a new kind of monastery on an island in the Tyrrhene Sea, Lérins, off the coast that is now known as the French Riviera. It was a high-powered seminary whose aim was to train dedicated and scholarly monastic clergy, and to persuade the cities of Gaul to choose them as bishops. Lérins succeeded, and among its most eminent monks were Hilary, who became bishop of Arles, the chief city of southern Gaul, and a young Briton named Faustus, who came to Lérins while Patrick was in Gaul, succeeded Hilary as abbot, and in time became bishop of Riez, in Provence; his extensive writings are the foundation of future Gallic theology. On the mainland the most forceful ally of Lérins from its early years was Germanus, a close friend of Hilary, who succeeded Amator at Auxerre in 418.

This was the Gaul in which Patrick won friends. The isolated statement attributed to him, that he visited Italy and the Tyrrhene islands, evidently Rome and Lérins, is quite possibly true. But they were not the most important places in his early life. Muirchu says that he set out for Rome, and on his way spent a long time with Germanus at Auxerre; he does not say whether or not the journey to Rome was ever completed. By Muirchu's time, tradition already made his sojourn at Auxerre last for 30 or 40 years, but one detail that Muirchu misunderstood gives à more exact indication of the time. He says that Germanus had Patrick consecrated bishop by Amator, an 'important bishop who lived nearby';[5] he had previously implied that Germanus consecrated him. He evidently used a source that mentioned consecration by bishop Amator, but did not state his see. Since Amator was Germanus' predecessor and died in 418, its meaning was plainly that he ordained Patrick as priest or deacon; evidently as deacon, since Patrick was hardly as old as 30, the minimum age for a priest, by 418.

Patrick was at Auxerre before 418, and finally left the city in 431 or 432. But his stay was not continuous. He himself says that the voice which commanded him in a dream to escape told him that he was to return to his homeland, and after his account of travel by sea and through deserted lands he continues 'again a few years later I was in Britain with my kinsfolk.'[6] It was evidently his first return after his captivity, for his kinsmen welcomed him and begged him never to leave home again after his tribulations. The 'few years' since he left Ireland had been spent abroad, at Auxerre, perhaps also at Rome and Lérins. But Patrick was resolved. In another dream he was visited by 'a man named Victoricus'[7] who urged him to return to Ireland and convert the heathen. The man was evidently Victricius of Rouen; Victricius is the only European ecclesiastic known to have urged or practised missions to the heathen and to have had an important following in Britain in the time of Patrick's father.

But Patrick could not go on his own. Muirchu reports that after the vision he left home and came to Germanus at Auxerre, who ultimately secured his appointment to Ireland. The appointment was entirely novel, for Victricius had on his own initiative preached to barbarians on the borders of his own diocese, but neither the Pope nor the bishops of Gaul had yet consecrated any bishop to any heathens beyond the frontiers of Rome. The decision was a by-product of more urgent ecclesiastical politics. One of the sequels to the shock of the fall of Rome in 410 had been the triumph of the views of the great African bishop, Augustine of Hippo, who rooted a disciplined, centralised church upon the doctrine that all men are from birth condemned by the sin of Adam, and may be saved only by the Grace of God, in practice bestowed by a sacrament, administered by a canonically ordained priest. Augustine's principal opponent was a British scholar long resident in Rome, Pelagius, acknowledged by his enemies as the most polished Latinist and most learned theologian of the day; until 410, Pelagius' old fashioned liberal views remained orthodox, but by 418 Augustine had triumphed, and Pelagians were condemned as heretics by rescripts issued by the imperial government. But in 410 the imperial government had renounced authority over Britain, and authorised the British to establish an independent government and look to their own defence. Rescripts issued in 418 were no longer valid in Britain, and the British church remained Pelagian, immune to the new doctrines of Augustine.

By the late 420s, British Pelagianism seemed a menace to the bishops of Gaul and to the Pope. In 429 'on the initiative of Deacon Palladius Pope Celestine sent bishop Germanus of Auxerre as his representative to confound the heretics and guide the British to the Catholic faith.'[8] The Chronicler Prosper, who reports the event, was a friend of Palladius, who was the Pope's personal deacon and possible successor. Germanus' biographer, who was also a well informed contemporary, a friend of Germanus' companion in Britain, reports the visit in detail and makes it sound as successful as he can; but though he claims widespread popular support for the visiting bishops, he is unable to cite any significant achievement of its aim; no synod condemned the heresy, or was even convened to hear the Pope's emissary, and no ecclesiastic is reported to have been deprived or to have changed his views, though Germanus' visit is said to have been approved by a convention of Gallic bishops.

When Germanus' visit brought no result, Rome took more drastic action. Prosper reports that in 431 Palladius came to the British Isles in person, with a stronger status than a papal envoy; the Pope conse- crated him as 'first bishop to the Irish Christians'.[9] The exceptional appointment emphasises the seriousness with which Rome took the problem; no Latin Pope had previously consecrated a bishop to any barbarians anywhere outside the empire, and the despatch of the principal priest of the city of Rome to a remote island was not prompted solely by new-found missionary zeal. Prosper's summary of Celestine's struggle against the Pelagians in Italy and elsewhere stresses the stronger motive; 'in consecrating a bishop to the Irish, while striving to keep the Roman island Catholic, he also made the barbarian island Christian.'[10] The first motive was the struggle against Pelagianism in Britain; the British bishops would not listen to the Pope's emissary, and in the 430s the Pope had no power to intrude a bishop into an existing British see. In creating a new see for the Irish, he was able to introduce an important orthodox leader among the heretics. But the new bishop also had to discharge the duties of his see; though Prosper exaggerates in claiming simply that he 'made Ireland Christian', he plainly visited Ireland and made some converts.

Palladius was appointed as bishop to Irishmen who were already Christian. They may have been numerous, for many Irish colonists had been settled for more than a generation in western Britain, most numerous in Demetia, modern Pembrokeshire, with parts of the adjoining counties; many are likely to have embraced the faith of their British neighbours, and to have made some converts among their kinsmen at home, most of whom lived in southern Ireland; and Irish tradition credits Palladius with several foundations in Leinster, the nearest coast to Pembrokeshire. The wording of Prosper's summary, published about 435, implies that Palladius was then dead; and shortly afterwards his office of papal deacon was filled by Leo, afterwards Pope Leo the Great. Irish tradition held that Palladius was ill-received, and left within the year, dying on his way back to Rome.

Muirchu relates that in the meantime Germanus had made a similar proposal. Some years before, Patrick had resolved to go to Ireland, and had attached himself to Germanus; he could not achieve his ambition without powerful support from established ecclesiastical authorities. Muirchu's account complements the contemporary notices of Prosper and of Germanus' biographer. Patrick himself says that his dreams of Victoricus' urging him to visit Ireland first came to him in

Britain, but could not be realised for many years. Muirchu says that he had many such dreams while in Auxerre; and he undoubtedly pressed Germanus to support him. Germanus in the end consented, and despatched Patrick, still a priest, in the care of a senior priest, when he heard of Palladius' appointment, which provided a 'suitable opportunity'.[11] But on their way, they heard of Palladius' death, and Patrick was then consecrated bishop in his place.

Patrick himself says that his appointment was approved, against considerable opposition, by a synod of British bishops. Some objected to his personal unsuitability, since his captivity had interrupted his education before his Latin was fluent, and left him semi-literate; for, like most men of his class in Britain, he was bilingual, speaking both his native tongue and Latin, but writing only in Latin, for British was unwritten. Others objected to the mission itself, asking what was the point of risking danger among enemy heathen. His family tearfully intreated him not go, offering public inducements.

The circumstances of the day explain his need to win the approval of the British clergy and the British government, and also explain the divided views that his intention aroused. The clergy had recently survived a papal attempt to plant among them an alien who was in their view an overbearing heretic. Patrick was no theologian; his writings show no trace of Pelagianism, but also no trace of Augustinianism. He was not only uninterested in theological controversy; he detested ecclesiastical politics, for they interfered with his single minded aim, his long cherished ambition to convert the Irish, whom he had come to love during his captivity. But he came to Britain as the nominee of Germanus and the successor of Palladius, heir to two continental bishops who had tried and failed to impose their authority over the British church. Patrick had to disprove the suspicion that he was a third alien intruder; his evident passionate sincerity proved that he was not to those who had met him, but it was not evident until they met him.

The despatch of a British bishop to the Irish also involved both governments.[12] The new ruler of Britain was Vortigern. He had recently enlisted a naval force of Saxons from the lower Elbe; Irish tradition reports that in the early 430s the Saxons raided the Irish coast and showed the potential strength of their fleet. Tradition also reports a treaty, sealed by a marriage alliance, between the Irish and British governments; its consequence was that Vortigern's overran and subdued the Irish colonists in western Britain without interference from Ireland. The Irish government was intimidated, and gave the British bishop grudging licence to preach without intimidation. The spread of Christianity in Ireland clearly suited the British government; but in Ireland Patrick appeared to conservative and established opinion as a hostile foreigner imposed by force, preaching the faith of the national enemy, and corrupting the youth; his was 'a strange and

troublesome doctrine . . . brought over seas from far away . . . that
would overthrow kingdoms . . . and destroy their gods'.[13]

Patrick struggled against enormous difficulties. He had first to
convince Roman churchmen that the conversion of heathen foreigners
was in itself desirable; he was suspect to his fellow clergy in Britain;
and in Ireland he appeared in the guise of an enemy agent. He over-
came the obstacles because his devotion defeated suspicion and his
resolution prevailed against threats and hostility. Muirchu's biography
pays particular attention to his first months in Ireland. He sailed up
the east coast, failing to find a welcome at several ports, and eventually
landed and made his headquarters at Saul, near Downpatrick, in
Ulster. There he tried to visit his former master, Miliucc, but was
thwarted by suspicion, for Miliucc committed suicide in fear at his
approach. He then made a direct challenge to the major national
religious festival at the royal centre of Tara, which coincided with the
Christian Easter; his resolute confrontation of the chief druids, or
magi, and his defiance of the High-King, earned him the nominal sub-
mission of constituted authority, and gave him continuing licence to
preach unhindered.

Patrick's own account outlines the sequel in general terms. He
travelled widely; he met persistent opposition from regional rulers,
and was imprisoned at least twice for short periods, but suffered no
greater violence. He made numerous converts, including the sons and
daughters of some local kings, and also some slaves, as well as free and
unfree persons of varying status in between. Often he had to pay
kings to grant permission for their children, subjects and slaves to
follow him; many of his converts, especially the women, took monastic vows; and he ordained several priests.

The crisis that stung Patrick into issuing his *Declaration* blew up
after he had been a dozen or more years in Ireland, when he was in his
late fifties. 'I was attacked by a number of my elders, who came and
brought up my sins against my arduous episcopate . . . After thirty
years they found a pretext . . . in a confession I had made before I was
a deacon . . . I had told a close friend what I had once done as a child
. . . God knows if I was fifteen years old at the time.'[14] The attack
came at last 30 years after his sin as a fifteen year old, perhaps 30
years after its confession; the probable date is about the early 440s.
The elders who made the attack were evidently British ecclesiastics,
for the single practical decision which Patrick announces is his refusal
to come to Britain; and he attaches to his refusal a warning that he
could also go on to visit the brethren in Gaul. He clearly refused a
request or demand. His appointment had originally been approved by
a synod of British bishops; another British synod now claimed
authority over the bishop of the Irish.

Patrick was again involved in ecclesiastical politics; he was bitterly
distressed at the conduct of his friend, to whom he had long ago

confessed his childish sin in confidence. The friend had none the less strongly supported him when he was endorsed as bishop, in 431 or 432; but had now turned against him, broken his confidence, revealed his confession, and used it impugn his fitness for his episcopate. Patrick's life's work was at stake. The reason he gave for his refusal to come to Britain was that he feared to waste the labour he had begun. He did not mean that all would be undone if he took a few weeks leave of absence, for his plea was that Christ had commanded him to be with the Irish for the rest of his life. He meant that if he admitted the authority of the British church by attending at their summons, he would be unlikely to return to Ireland, and risked replacement. But he did not trust the British bishops to win the confidence of his Irish converts. They were 'intellectual clerics',[15] products of the opulent gentlemanly society of Roman Britain, whose elegance and subtlety had offended Germanus in 429; and many of them regarded the Irish simply as enemy barbarians. They were naturally suspect to the Irish; Patrick's own rustic simplicity had broken down suspicion, but other British clergy, less sympathetic in their outlook, caused trouble. The earliest list of ecclesiastical regulations of the Irish Church, known as the *Canons of St. Patrick*, is probably in essence the work of Patrick and his clergy in the middle of the fifth century; it includes a rule that forbids British clergy to preach in Ireland without licence from the Irish church, and the rule was clearly devised in the light of experience. The Irish church had need of British clerics, and several of those named as Patrick's younger contemporaries in the late fifth century were British by name and birth; but Patrick and his colleagues needed to be able to choose those who were temperamentally suited to their task, and to reject the unfit. It may well be that Patrick's rejection of unsuitable British clergy had been the occasion of the dispute, the reason that prompted the British church to assert authority.

Patrick rejected the metropolitan claims of the British episcopate. Something of the sequel is outlined in the terse notices of the Irish Annals and in Muirchu. Under the pontificate of Leo the Great (440-461), the Annals note his 'approval' (*probatio*) of Patrick. The word is no technical canonical term, and does not concern Patrick's theology, which was never in dispute; and the surviving abbreviated transcripts of the Annals knew nothing of its context. It is a simple ordinary word, meaning no more and no less than it says. The Pope approved Patrick's episcopate in Ireland. Patrick's own *Declaration* and Pope Leo's policy elsewhere combine to give the general and particular context. The bishops of Britain witheld approval and claimed supremacy over the Irish church, and Patrick threatened to appeal over their heads to Gaul, where his old patron Germanus was now the senior bishop, in frequent contact with Rome. Leo's principal ecclesiastical endeavour was to assert the direct authority of Rome over individual sees, and to diminish the authority of provincial synods and metropolitans; the bitterest dispute of his pontificate was with Hilary of Arles, metropolitan of the Gauls, over the right of appointment to a Gallic see. When the Irish and British churches were in dispute, Leo could not do otherwise than approve the independence of the Irish church from Britain, and assert its direct dependence upon Rome. The notice of the *probatio* places it only within the 20 years of Leo's pontificate; but an additional entry may indicate a more precise date, for under the year 443 the Annals enter, without explanation, the short comment 'Patrick flourished'. It may mark the year when Leo recognised the independence of the Irish church.

Two of the embroidered tales in Muirchu have some external confirmation, and both indicate a widening of Patrick's activity after his approval. At an unspecified date he is said to have installed one of his Irish converts as bishop of the Isle of Man, with the participation of two bishops with British names.[16] The story is muddled, but its reality rests upon the two other bishops; for the consecration of a new bishop required the laying on of hands by at least three existing bishops, and Patrick could not by himself consecrate bishops. He needed the collaboration of two sympathetically minded British bishops.

The second story is of greater moment. The Annals date the foundation of Armagh to 444, the year after the likely date of Patrick's independence. Armagh is situated within short walking distance of Emain, now Navan Fort, the ancient holy centre of the Ulaid kings, who are said to have been expelled thence soon after 300, and replaced by the new dynasty of the Airgialla. Muirchu gives a detailed circumstantial account of Patrick's vigorous insistence on the Armagh site.[17] The regional Airgialla ruler, Daire, offered him a site at the foot of the hill, but Patrick demanded the hill top, which in Irish was known as Daire's Fortress; and after very considerable pressure, he obtained it, and built his church thereon.

Two items of circumstantial evidence bear upon Muirchu's story. The tradition of the Irish genealogists lists the kings of the local dynasty, and names the mid-fifth century ruler Daire; but they are wholly unaware that he was the Daire of Muirchu's story, though they meticulously note other kings who were reputed to have granted the lands upon which other major monasteries were built. Their tradition is wholly independent of the legends of Patrick and Armagh and of Muirchu's account, but it concurs in naming the same king at the same time and place.

The second item is a more recent archaeological discovery. Excavation in the churchyard of Armagh has revealed that the hill-top was in fact fortified; carbon dating of the rapid silt from its defensive ditch indicates that the fort was constructed within a few decades of 300, at about the time when Daire's ancestors are said to have deprived the Ulaid of half their territory, including their ancient centre at nearby Emain.

Muirchu describes the foundation of Armagh at length and with emphasis; but he does not assert that it became Patrick's principal centre. On the contrary, all reports agree that he remained at Downpatrick, and there died. His first and permanent headquarters were located in the lands that the Ulaid had retained, near to one of their chief royal residences. Armagh was founded at the centre of a neighbouring kingdom, a decade after Patrick had established himself among the Ulaid. But it became the seat of his acknowledged successors, and was early accorded a primacy among the later sees of Christian Ireland, its bishop named first in papal letters addressed to the Irish bishops.

In his later years, Patrick wrote his *Letter* of protest to king Coroticus; it followed an earlier lost letter, that had been delivered by a priest whom Patrick had trained since childhood, and was therefore despatched when he had lived some 20 or 25 years in Ireland. The name Coroticus is one of the commonest, oldest and longest lived names used by the British and Welsh; it was first recorded at the time of the Roman conquest of Britain, in the first century AD, and was then spelt Caratacus by the Roman historian Tacitus; its later spellings include Ceredig, Cerdic and Caradauc, and it remains in modern use as Caradog. Muirchu names Coroticus as king of Ail (i.e. of Dumbarton, on the Clyde); and the British genealogies independently report a Clyde king of that name in the mid fifth century; Muirchu adds that he was soon after struck down by the hand of the Lord for his offence against Patrick. His ships had raided the Irish coasts, seizing prisoners whom they sold as slaves to the Picts and heathen Irish, probably Irish colonists in western Scotland. The prisoners included recently baptised converts, whom the raiders refused to return. The coasts concerned were evidently within easy reach of the Clyde; Patrick was still active in Ulster.

The several texts of the Annals give the date of Patrick's death as 17 March 459, and various texts indicate that he was between 60 and 63 when he died; the latter age is more probable, since he reached Auxerre not later than 418, and he says himself that he was about 22 at the time. He was therefore born not later than 396. His death left a vacuum that only Rome could fill, for there were no other bishops in Ireland to consecrate a successor, and the British bishops were no longer responsible for the Irish see. Appropriate measures were taken. Half a dozen northern Irish bishops are recorded in the generation after Patrick's death, each established in a separate kingdom, most of them resident within walking distance, or a short drive, of a royal centre. Few of the new bishops' seats became permanent sees, but they marked a first adaptation of Roman ecclesiastical organisation to a barbarian land. Roman practice had always established bishoprics at the centres of lay political authority; and within the Roman empire such centres had been cities. Ireland had no cities; its political centres were royal forts, and the importance and boundaries of the several kingdoms were still in a state of rapid change. The sees of the late fifth century represented only the political realities of that generation, and the regions in which Christians were numerous enough to warrant a bishop. The creation of a number of sees enabled future bishops to be consecrated at home; and whatever canonical authority they possessed necessarily rested upon the approval of the Pope, either of Leo, who died in 461, or of his successor, Hilary.

No source reports the foundation of the northern sees; only their existence is recorded, usually at the death of each bishop. The traditions of the south are, however, clear and emphatic. Four sees, each in a principal kingdom, each wholly independent of Patrick, were held to have been founded simultaneously, between 461 and 468, by Pope Hilary, who consecrated the first bishops in Rome, and was assisted by prominent ecclesiastics of western Britain, whose guidance the Irish shortly afterwards rejected. All these tales agree that Christians were then few in southern Ireland, and priests rare and hard to find. A few monasteries are also recorded, but women's houses were far more prominent than men's.

Christianity seized hold of Irish society in the decades after 530. Its impetus and model came from a reformed British church, whose novel structure was welcomed in Ireland; and was inspired by the example of St. Benedict in Italy. The civil society of Roman Britain, that had bred the genteel urban bishops whom Patrick criticised, was swept away in the second half of the fifth century, in the course of a long war against the Saxons, or English; and the aftermath of the war left a corrupt and servile episcopate, dependent upon the pleasure of warlord kings, detested by rich and poor, cleric and layman. In reaction, south-western Britain was swept by a monastic movement, that for the first time in Europe matched the scale of the original monastic upsurge in Egypt, 200 years earlier. The Irish also suffered from the uncontrolled ferocity of upstart local dynasties, and immediately adopted monasticism as enthusiastically as the British. Abbots quickly inherited the popular respect that had formerly been paid to Druids, and Irish Christianity was rooted on monasteries and identified with them. The episcopalian church of Patrick and his successors continued, governed by rules that provided for an ordinary married secular clergy, as was then normal in the Roman church. But it was overshadowed; the bishop and priest were reduced to the status of ecclesiastical officials, necessary for the performance of certain specified ritual functions, baptism, confirmation, marriage, burial and other sacraments. From the sixth century onwards, most of the recorded bishops were monks, detached from their abbeys to serve the needs of the laity. As monks, they remained subject to the authority of their abbot, whose superior rank was so marked that Irish idiom commonly described the Pope as 'abbot of Rome' and Christ as 'abbot of Heaven'.

The peculiarities of the Irish church did not disturb Europe so long as they were confined to Ireland. But Irish missionary zeal was continuously renewed, and soon spilled abroad. In the middle of the seventh century, Irish monks converted the Northumbrian and midland English, who then held suzerainty over the south; and monasteries on the Irish model were permanently implanted upon the English in large numbers. Irish and English monks emigrated in large numbers to Europe, where their fervent piety aroused a response as enthusiastic as at home. Monasteries were founded in large numbers in eastern Gaul, with a few in Italy, by Irish and English immigrants and their native converts, and English and Irish monks successfully undertook the conversion of the pagan Germans and Slavs beyond the Rhine to Christianity.

The eruption of the Irish church into Europe brought its differences from Rome into sharp and controversial focus. Rome demanded conformity. Dispute was wisely centred upon externals, notably the method of calculating the date of Easter, and the form of the tonsure; concentration upon the relatively simple external issues enabled common-sense flexible compromise to be reached upon the essentials, particularly upon ecclesiastical organisation, upon the relation of abbot and bishop to each other and to Rome, and upon the relation of monk and layman to the priest and God.

Each country worked out with time and difficulty its own solution. Among the English, the remains of Roman towns enabled archbishop Theodore to establish an urban see in each main kingdom, and to achieve harmonious relations between bishops, abbots and kings; in most of Wales, where Roman towns were few, the abbots of principal monasteries were accepted simultaneously as the bishops of main kingdoms. But the problems of Ireland were more complicated; and their solution caused the revival and elevation of Patrick's memory.

The ecclesiastical conflicts of the seventh century reflected the ancient antagonism of the north and the south, between Conn's Half (Connaught and Ulster, with Meath), and Mog's Half (Munster and Leinster). The adherents of conformity with Rome quickly won a large following in the south, for Irishmen who frequently travelled to Europe soon learnt the practical disadvantages of insular eccentricity; but the spread of Romanism in the south hardened conservatism in the north. The southerners soon realised that their episcopate was out of step with Europe because their many sees were unfixed, and their bishops owed no allegiance to a metropolitan archbishop, but were each subject to their own abbot.

The first attempt at organisational conformity was advanced by Muirchu's father, Cogitosus, about 650 or a little earlier. He published a biography of Brigit of Kildare in Leinster, the principal saint of the south. His preface proclaims that her bishop, Conlaed, with his heirs after him, was properly 'archbishop of all the churches of Ireland from sea to sea'.[18]

The claim of a Leinster bishop, dependent upon a powerful abbess, to be archbishop of all Ireland had no chance of acceptance in the north, and is not again repeated. But shortly afterwards another Leinster bishop, Aed of Sletty, advanced a subtler and more practicable proposal. He placed his own church under the suzerainty of Armagh. He was a leading advocate of conformity with Rome, and the initiative that presented a northern see, in the centre of conservative resistance, at the head of the conformist movement, was an effective step in winning northern agreement. An immediate by-product of Aed's initiative was Muirchu's biography; for Muirchu asserts that he wrote under the direction of Aed and at his command.

Muirchu's *Life of Patrick* was written in the early stages of the campaign to win the north, and made no extravagant claims. In a plain factual narrative, as accurate as half forgotten memories could permit, he focussed attention upon a single self-evident truth, that the Irish church had been founded by Patrick, long before the time of the monasteries; and that Patrick was a properly consecrated Roman bishop, trained by the orthodox Germanus, appointed as the immediate and legitimate successor of Palladius, whom the Pope had personally consecrated. His narrative concentrates upon Patrick's origins and arrival and is simplified by reaching a climax with Patrick's triumph at Tara, the traditional centre of the High King of Ireland. The account of the High King's formal conversion did duty for the conversion of Ireland and avoided much troublesome further detail.

The Leinster initiative succeeded, and effective agreement with the north was reached at a synod convened at Birr in central Ireland in 697, under the presidency of Adomnan, abbot of Iona and biographer of Columba, at which Aed, Muirchu, and many northern ecclesiastics were present. The Romanists prevailed, but their triumph took long to consolidate. Several churchmen and monasteries long witheld consent; even Adomnan failed to persuade his own monks, who did not yield for another 20 years.

Consolidation needed more forceful argument. Muirchu went on to stress the foundation of Armagh. It was the centre of Patrician tradition, for no important permanent monastery remained at Patrick's own headquarters at Saul, and Armagh was his only other known important personal foundation. But the organisation of a hierarchy under a metropolitan archbishop of Armagh required much more forceful and colourful argument than Muirchu's sober historical narrative. The pioneer of Armagh's wide claim was a contemporary Connaught cleric, Tirechan. His work begins with a very brief condensed summary of Muirchu's narrative, or of Muirchu's sources, and proceeds to audacious assertions, claiming that Patrick was responsible for the foundation of all churches throughout Ireland that did not belong to the major monasteries, and of many that did. He opens with the direct statement that Patrick consecrated 450 bishops and innumerable priests, though neither Patrick himself nor Muirchu suggests that he consecrated any bishops in Ireland; and by himself he had not the power to consecrate any. The rest of the work consists of a long list of churches, set in the framework of a mythical journey of Patrick through Ireland. The method is simple and uniform. Tirechan reports the tradition of each church about its own founders, and makes Patrick baptise them, bless them in youth, foretell their greatness, or otherwise assume responsibility for their foundation. The conclusion is that all these churches owed their origin to Patrick, and should therefore accept the supremacy of his successor at Armagh.

Tirechan's purpose is roundly stated. 'If Patrick's heir should claim his parish, he could recover almost the whole island, for God gave it him . . . for his are all the early churches of Ireland'. But he admits that the claim is not believed by contemporaries, for his heart was troubled to see that 'deserters and rogues and military men bear hatred to the parish of Patrick, since they have taken from it what was his.'[19] The 'deserters and rogues' were churchmen who did not admit the claims of Patrick's heir at Armagh, and denied the truth of Tirechan's assertions. They were of course right. Patrick did not consecrate 450, or 50 or any other number of bishops; and most of the people whom Tirechan makes him meet were not born until long after his death.

It is a well known axiom of political deceit that if a lie is to be believed, it must be an outrageous untruth, conceived on a grand scale. Tirechan's pretence was as widely accepted as Geoffrey of Monmouth's pretended History of Britain, and has held sway over men's minds even longer. It was followed in succeeding centuries by a riot of even wilder invention elaborating upon his theme. The earlier of these texts were bound together in the Book of Armagh at the beginning of the 9th century, and became the sacred foundation of the claims of the see. They have ever since pervaded, corrupted and obscured the straight-forward reality of his life and work, and would have altogether submerged him if the Armagh Book had not also preserved his own works.

The general body of falsehood produced many significant side-currents. One of the more pernicious was an exercise of pedantic Irish scholarship concerning Patrick's age. It began with a figure that the mid-seventh century hermit Constans of Lough Oughter in County Cavan 'discovered in Gaul', to the effect that Patrick 'taught for 61 years'.[20] It was evidently originally a note of his age at death. To it was added the figure, already known to Muirchu, that he studied for 40 years, clearly originally meaning the lapse of time between his arrival at Auxerre and his death. The further addition of the 20 odd years of youth before he reached Auxerre gave a round figure total of 120 years. By the end of the 7th century, a note attached to

Tirechan's book pointed out that this was also the age of Moses; and simple division divided Patrick's life into 60 years spent before he reached Ireland, and 60 in Ireland.

These abtruse calculations were soon incorporated into the tradition of the annalists. Their arid calculation subtracted 120 years from Patrick's death date, at about 460, and entered his birth at about 340, while another scholar added the 60 years of his life in Ireland to the date of his arrival in 432, to achieve an additional death date at 493. Most Annals thenceforth carried two alternative dates for Patrick's death, and prompted the intelligent Tirechan, or his annotator, to infer that since two different dates were given, there must have been two Patricks,[21] of whom the earlier should be identified with Palladius, the later with the Patrick who landed in 432 and died in 493.

Such mechanical quirks are a normal part of early medieval scholarship. But they experienced an unusual and bizarre revival in the 1940s and 1950s, when a variety of conflicting theories solemnly resurrected the two Patricks, each theory selecting such limited portions of the available evidence as suited its conclusion. These curious speculations, largely confined to Ireland, were scrutinised in a magisterial article in 1962 which exposed their fragile argumentation.[22]

The mass of rubbish that has been piled about the memory of Patrick in ancient and modern times has done little positive harm, for Patrick is his own truthful witness, and Muirchu was a sober biographer. But negative damage has been considerable. Because the extravagance of Tirechan and his successors has been taken as serious evidence for the life of Patrick, who remains the patron saint of Ireland, their true importance has been undervalued; for though they contribute nothing but untruth and distortion to the study of Patrick and the fifth century, they are contemporary texts of the first importance for the history of 7th and 8th century Ireland and its beliefs. They take their place beside a great quantity of secular texts, of equal importance, but equally little studied. These texts deserve full examination, for in these centuries the detailed history of Ireland is considerably better documented than the history of England, or of most European countries; these are the years when Ireland was in the course of transformation from an alien barbarian island into a European nation, and in which all Europe was deeply indebted to the ferment of ideas that poured from Ireland. The neglected texts, misused for the wrong purpose, require proper consideration. They form a proper and significant part of the study of the formation of medieval Europe.

All this literature, important in its own right and its proper context, must be cleared away from the study of Patrick. His own writings and Muirchu's Life, combined with what else is known of the age in which he lived, together give a clear outline of his life and work. To understand them, it is necessary to explain their context and to remove the irrelevance and confusion that hides them. When they can be seen in their own right, Patrick's own awkward language speaks for itself. His courage and his fears, his resolution and his hesitations, his persistent devotion to a people whom he knew, understood and loved, and his determination to do all he could for their well-being on earth and hereafter, in disregard of all obstacles and all other considerations, are utterly remote from the ecclesiastical portrait of a plaster saint and a national idol. He is one of the few personalities of fifth century Europe who has revealed himself with living warmth, in terms that men of any age who care for their fellows can comprehend. He is no more typical of his time than any other man in any other time; but through the eyes of Patrick men may penetrate beyond the headlines and the generalities of historians ancient and modern, may perceive something of the human problems that are common to their age and his and also something of the essential differences that distinguish one age from the other. Patrick's moving and intensely personal account of his life and troubles is much more than a story of the conversion of the Irish to Christianity; it touches the mainsprings of human endeavour and teaches not only the history of one period, but the substance of what history is about.

NOTES

1. For further discussion of the historical evidence see J. Morris 'The dates of the Celtic Saints' *Journal of Theological Studies* N.S. 17 (1966), 342 - 391; and, more generally, J. Morris *The Age of Arthur* (London, 1973). Other treatments of the controversies surrounding Patrick are most easily accessible in the following: L. Bieler *The Life and Legend of St. Patrick* (Dublin, 1948); D. A. Binchy 'Patrick and his biographers' *Studia Hibernica* 2 (1962), 7 - 173; R. P. C. Hanson *St. Patrick: his Origins and Career* (Oxford, 1968).
2. J. F. Kenney *Sources for the Early History of Ireland* (New York, 1929), p. 324.
3. *Dicta* 1.
4. Sulpicius Severus *Vita S. Martini* 9.
5. Muirchu 1.9.
6. *Confessio* 23.
7. *Confessio* 23.
8. Prosper of Aquitaine *Chronicle*, ed. Mommsen: M.G.H. Auct. Ant. ix, p.472.
9. *Ibid.*, p. 473.
10. Prosper of Aquitaine *Contra Collatorem* 21 (PL 51.271).
11. Muirchu 1.8.
12. cf. J. Morris *The Age of Arthur*, pp. 62-66.
13. Muirchu 1.10.
14. *Confessio* 26-27.
15. *Confessio* 13.
16. Muirchu 1.23.
17. Muirchu 1.25.
18. Cogitosus *Vita S. Brigittae*: Acta Sanctorum Feb. i, p. 135.
19. Tirechan *Collectanea*: Book of Armagh, fol. 11 a 2; ed. Hogan *Analecta Bollandiana* 2 (1883), pp. 45-46.
20. Book of Armagh, fol. 8 b 2; ed. Hogan *Analecta Bollandiana* 1 (1882),p.584.
21. Tirechan *Collectanea*: Book of Armagh, fol. 16 a 1; ed. Hogan, p. 67.
22. D. A. Binchy *Studia Hibernica* 2 (1962), pp. 7-173.

MUIRCHÚ'S LIFE OF ST PATRICK

edited and translated by A. B. E. Hood

TEXT

Asterisks direct the reader to textual notes on pp. 119–21.

Preface

Quoniam quidem, mi domine Aido, multi conati sunt ordinare narrationem utique istam secundum quod patres eorum et qui ministri ab initio fuerunt sermonis tradiderunt illis, sed propter difficillimum narrationis opus diversasque opiniones et plurimorum plurimas suspiciones nunquam ad unum certumque historiae tramitem pervenierunt; ideo, ni fallor, iuxta hoc nostrorum proverbium, ut deducuntur pueri in ambiteathrum, in hoc periculossum et profundum narrationis sanctae pylagus, turgentibus proterve gurgitum aggeribus, inter acutissimos carubdes per ignota aequora insitos, a nullis adhuc lintribus, excepto tantum uno patris mei Coguitosi, * expertum atque occupatum, ingenioli mei puerilem remi cymbam deduxi. Sed ne magnum de parvo videar finguere, pauca haec de multis sancti Patricii gestis parva peritia, incertis auctoribus, memoria labili, attrito sensu, vili sermone, sed affectu piissimo caritatis, sanctitatis tuae et auctoritatis imperio oboediens, carptim gravatimque explicare aggrediar.

1 De ortu Patricii et eius prima captivitate.
2 De navigio eius cum gentibus et vexatione diserti et cibo sibi et gentilibus divinitus delato.
3 De secunda captura, quam senis decies diebus ab inimicis pertulerat.
4 De susceptione sua a parentibus ubi agnoverunt eum.
5 De aetate eius quando iens videre sedem apostolicam voluit discere sapientiam.
6 De inventione sancti Germani in Galliis, et ideo non exivit ultra.
7 De aetate eius quando vissitavit eum anguelus ut veniret adhuc.
8 De reversione eius de Gallis et ordinatione Palladii et mox morte eius.
9 De ordinatione eius ab Amathorege episcopo, defuncto Palladio.
10 De rege gentili †habeto† in Temoria quando venerat sanctus Patricius babtismum portans.
11 De primo eius itenere in hac insola ut seipsum redemeret o Miliucc priusquam alios a demonio traheret.
12 De morte Milcon et verbo Patricii de semine eius.
13 De consilio sancti Patricii ubi hessitum est de celebratione primi paschae.

Haec pauca de sancti Patricii peritia et virtutibus Muirchu maccu Machtheni, dictante Aiduo Slebtiensis civitatis episcopo, conscripsit.

1 Patricius, qui et Sochet vocabatur, Brito natione, in Britannis natus, Cualfarnio diacono ortus, filio, ut ipse ait, Potiti presbyteri, qui fuit vico Bannavem Taburniae, haud procul a mari nostro, quem vicum constanter indubitanterque comperimus esse † ventre †*, matre etiam conceptus Concessa nomine.
Annorum xvi. puer cum ceteris captus, in hanc barbarorum insulam advectus est et apud quendam gentilem immitemque regem in servitute detentus. Qui sexennium more Hebraico ⟨in ea captivitate exegit⟩*, cum timore Dei et tremore, secundum psalmiste sententiam, in vigiliis et orationibus multis. Cencies in die et cencies in nocte orabat, libenter reddens ⟨quae Dei sunt Deo et quae Caesaris Caesari⟩*, incipiensque timere Deum et amare omnipotentem

Dominum; nam usque ad id temporis ignorabat Deum verum, sed tunc spiritus fervebat in eo.

Post multas ibi tribulationes, post famem et sitim, post frigora et nuditates, post pascenda pecora, post frequentias angeli Victorici a Deo ad illum missi, post magnas virtutes omnibus pene notas, post responsa divina (e quibus unum aut duo haec exempli tantum gracia demonstrabo: 'Bene ieiunas, cito iturus ad patriam tuam;' et iterum: 'Ecce navis tua parata est;' quae non erat prope, sed forte habebat ducenta milia passuum, ubi numquam habuerat iter) — post haec omnia, ut diximus, quae enumerari poene a nemine possunt, cum ignotis barbaris gentilibusque hominibus multos et falsos deos adorantibus iam in nave sibi parata, deserto terreno gentilique rege* cum actibus suis et accepto caelesti eternoque Deo, in comitatu sancti Spiritus ex praecepto divino* aetatis suae anno xxiii. ad Britanias navigavit.

2   Ternis itaque diebus totidemque noctibus quasi ad modum Ionae in mari cum iniquis fluctuans, postea bis denis simul et octenis diurnis luminibus Moysico more, alio licet sensu, per desertum fatigatus, murmurantibus gentilibus quasi Iudei fame et siti pene deficientibus, compulsus a gubernatore, temptatus atque ut illis Deum suum ne perirent oraret rogatus, mortalibus exoratus, turmae misertus, spiritu contribulatus, merito coronatus, a Deo magnificatus, abundantiam cibi ex grege porcorum a Deo misso sibi velut ex coturnicum turma Deo adiuvante prebuit. Mel quoque silvestre ut quondam Iohanni subvenit, motatis tamen pessimorum gentilium merito porcinis carnibus pro locustarum usu. Ille autem sanctus Patricius nichil gustans de his cibis, immolaticum enim erat, nec esuriens nec sitiens mansit illesus. Eadem vero nocte dormiens, temptavit eum satanas graviter, fingens saxa ingentia et quasi comminuens iam membra eius; sed invocato Helia bina voce, ortus est ei sol qui refulgens expulit omnes caliginum tenebras et restitutae sunt ei vires eius.

3   Et iterum post multos annos capturam ab alienigenis pertulit. Ubi prima nocte audire meruit responsum divinum sibi dicens: 'Duobus mensibus eris cum illis, id est cum inimicis tuis.' Quod ita factum est. Sexagesimo enim die liberavit eum Dominus de manibus eorum, previdens ei cum comitibus suis cibum et ignem et siccitatem quottidie, donec decimo die pervenerunt ad homines.

4   Et iterum post paucos annos ut antea in patria sua propria apud parentes suos requievit, qui ut filium receperunt, rogantes illum ut vel sic post tantas tribulationes et temptationes de reliquo vitae numquam ab illis discederet. Sed ille non consensit. Et ibi ostensae

sunt ei multae visiones.

5   Et erat annorum triginta, secundum apostolum 'in virum perfectum
     ⟨occurrens, in mensuram aetatis⟩* plenitudinis Christi.' Egressus
     ad sedem apostolicam visitandam et honorandam, ad caput utique*
     omnium ecclesiarum totius mundi, ut sapientiam divinam* sanctaque
     misteria ad quae vocavit illum Deus disceret atque intellegeret et
     impleret, et ut predicaret et donaret divinam gratiam in nationibus
     externis convertens ad fidem Christi.

6   Transnavigato igitur mari dextro Britannico ac coepto itinere per
     Gallias*, Alpes ad extremum, ut corde proposuerat, transcensurus,
     quendam sanctisimum episcopum Alsiodori civitate principem
     Germanum, ⟨Galliarum paene omnium⟩ summum dominum*,
     invenit. Aput quem non parvo tempore demoratus, iuxta id quod
     Paulus ad pedes Gamaliel fuerat, in omni subiectione et patientia
     atque oboedientia scientiam, sapientiam castitatemque et omnem
     utilitatem tam spiritus quam animae cum magno Dei timore et amore,
     in bonitate et simplicitate cordis, corpore et spiritu virgo,* toto animi
     desiderio didicit, dilexit, custodivit.

7   Peractisque* ibi multis temporibus quasi, ut alii, quadraginta, alii,
     triginta annis, ille antiquitus amicus valde fidelis*, Victoricus nomine,
     qui omnia sibi in Hibernica servitute possito antequam essent dixerat,
     eum crebris vissionibus vissitavit, dicens ei adesse tempus ut veniret
     et aevanguelico rete nationes feras et barbaras, ad quas docendas
     misserat illum Deus, ut piscaret; ibique ei dictum est in vissione:
     'Vocant te filii et filiae silvae Foclitae;' et caetera.

8   Oportuno ergo tempore imperante, comitante divino auxilio, coeptum
     ingreditur iter ad opus in quod ollim preparatus fuerat, utique
     aevanguelii. Et missit Germanus seniorem cum ullo, hoc est Segitium
     prespiterum, ut testem et comitem haberet, quia nec adhuc a sancto
     domino Germano in pontificali gradu ordinatus est. Certi etenim erant*
     quod Palladius, archidiaconus pape Caelestini urbis Romae episcopi,
     qui tunc tenebat sedem apostolicam quadragensimus quintus a sancto
     Petro apostolo, ille Palladius ordinatus et missus fuerat ad hanc insolam
     sub brumali rigore possitam convertendam. Sed prohibuit illum Deus*,
     quia nemo potest accipere quicquam de terra nisi datum ei fuerit de
     caelo. Nam neque hii feri et inmites homines facile receperunt
     doctrinam eius, neque et ipse voluit transegere tempus in terra non
     sua; sed reversus est ad eum qui missit illum. Revertente vero eo hinc
     et primo mari transito coeptoque terrarum itenere, in Britonum*
     finibus vita functus est.*

9   Audita itaque morte sancti Paladii in Britannis, quia discipuli Paladii,
    id est Augustinus et Benedictus et caeteri, redeuntes retulerant in
    Ebmoria de morte eius, Patricius et qui cum eo erant declinaverunt
    iter ad quendam mirabilem hominem summum episcopum,
    Amathoregem nomine, in propinquo loco habitantem. Ibique sanctus
    Patricius, sciens quae eventura erant illi,* episcopalem gradum ab
    Amathorege sancto episcopo accepit; sed etiam Auxilius Iserninusque
    et caeteri inferioris gradus eodem die quo sanctus Patricius ordinatus
    est. Tum acceptis benedictionibus, perfectisque omnibus secundum
    morem, cantato etiam Patricio quasi specialiter et convenienter hoc
    psalmistae vorsu: 'Tu es sacerdos in aeternum secundum ordinem
    Melchesedec;' venerabilis viator paratam navim in nomine sanctae
    Trinitatis ascendit et pervenit Brittannias; et omissis omnibus ambul-
    andi anfractibus praeter commone viae officium (nemo enim dissidia
    quaerit Dominum), cum omni velocitate flatuque prospero mare
    nostrum contendit.

10 In illis autem diebus quibus haec gesta sunt in praedictis regionibus
    fuit rex quidam magnus, ferox gentilisque imperator barbarorum
    regnans in Temoria, quae erat caput Scotorum, Loiguire nomine, filius
    Neill, origo stirpis regiae totius paene * insolae. Hic autem scivos et
    magos et aurispices et incantatores et omnis malae artis inventores
    habuerat, qui poterant omnia scire et providere ex more gentilitatis
    et idolatriae antequam essent; e quibus hii duo prae caeteris praefere-
    bantur, quorum nomina haec sunt, Lothroch qui et Lochru, et
    Lucetmael qui et Ronal.

    Et hii duo ex sua arte magica crebrius profetabant morem quendam
    exterum futurum in modum regni cum ignota quadam doctrina
    molesta de* longuinquo trans maria advectum, a paucis dictatum, a
    multis susceptum, ab omnibusque honoratum, regna subversurum,
    resistentes reges occisurum*, turbas seducturum, omnes eorum deos
    distructurum, et eiectis omnibus illorum artis opibus in saecula regnat-
    urum. Portantem quoque suadentemque hunc morem signaverunt et
    profetaverunt hiis verbis quasi in modum versiculi crebro ab hiisdem
    dictis, maxime in antecedentibus adventum Patricii duobus aut tribus
    annis. Haec autem sunt versiculi verba, propter linguae idioma* non
    tam manifesta:
    'Adveniet Asciciput cum suo ligno† curvicipite et sua domu capite
    perforata.†* Incantabit nefas a sua mensa ex anteriore parte domus
    suae; respondebit ei sua familia tota:"Fiat, fiat." ' (Quod nostris
    verbis potest manifestius exprimi). 'Quando ergo haec omnia fient,
    regnum nostrum, quod est gentile, non stabit.'

Quod sic postea evenerat. Eversis enim in adventu Patricii idulorum culturis, fides Christi catholica nostra replevit omnia. De his ista sufficiant; redeamus ad propossitum.

11 Consummato igitur navigio sancto perfectoque, honerata navis sancti cum transmarinis mirabilibus spiritalibusque tessauris, quasi in oportunum portum, in regiones Coolennorum in portum apud nos clarum, qui vocatur Hostium Dee, dilata est. Ubi vissum est ei nihil perfectius esse quam ut semetipsum primitus redemeret, et inde appetens sinistrales fines ad illum hominem gentilem Milcoin apud quem quondam in captivitate fuerat, portansque ei geminum servitutis pretium, terrenum utique et caeleste, ut de captivitate liberaret illum cui ante captivus servierat, ad anteriorem insolam, quae eius nomine usque hodie nominatur, prurim navis convertit. Tum de inde Brega Conalneosque fines, necnon et fines Ulathorum in levo dimitiens, ad extremum in* fretum quod est Brene se inmisit. Et descenderunt in terram ad hostium Slain ille et qui cum eo erant in navi, et absconderunt naviculam, et venierunt aliquantulum in regionem ut requiescerent ibi.

Et invenit eos porcinarius cuiusdam viri natura boni, licet gentilis, cui nomen erat Dichu, habitans ibi ubi nunc est Orreum Patricii nomine cognominatum. Porcinarius autem putans eos fures ac latrones, exivit et indicavit domino suo Dudichoin et induxit illum super eos ignorantibus illis. Qui corde propossuerat occidere eos, sed videns faciem sancti Patricii, convertit Dominus ad bonum cogitationes eius. Et praedicavit Patricius fidem illi, et ibi credidit Patricio, et requievit ibi sanctus apud illum non multis diebus.

Sed volens cito ire ut vissitaret praedictum hominem Milcoin et portaret ei pretium suum et vel sic converteret ad Christi fidem, relicta ibi navis apud Dichoin, coepit per terras diregere viam in regiones Cruidnenorum donec pervenit ad montem Miss. De quo monte multo ante, tempore quo ibi captivus servierat, presso vestigio in petra alterius montis, expedito gradu vidit angelum Victoricum in conspectu eius ascendisse in caelum.

12 Audiens autem Miliucc servum suum iterum venire* ad vissitandum eum, ut morem quem nolebat in fine vitae faceret quasi per vim, ne servo subiectus fieret et ille sibi dominaret, instinctu diabuli sponte se igni tradidit et in domu in qua prius habitaverat rex, congregato ad se omni instrumento substantiae suae, incensus est.

Stans autem sanctus Patricius in praedicto loco a latere dextero montis

Miss, ubi primum illam regionem in qua servivit cum tali gratia adveniens vidit (ubi nunc usque crux habetur in signum), ad vissum primum
illius regionis ilico sub oculis rogum regis incensum intuitus. Stupe-
factus igitur ad hoc opus duabus aut tribus fere horis nullum verbum
proferens, suspirans et gemens lacrimansque atque haec verba
promens ait: 'Nescio, Deus scit, hic homo rex qui se ipsum igni
tradidit ne crederet in fine vitae suae et ne serviret Deo aeterno, nescio,
Deus scit, nemo de filiis eius sedebit rex super sedem regni eius a
generatione in generationem; insuper et semen eius serviet in sempit-
ernum.'

Et his dictis, orans et armans se signo crucis, convertit cito iter suum
ad regionem Ulothorum per eadem vestigia quibus venerat, et rursum
pervenit in campum Inis ad Dichoin; ibique mansit diebus multis et
circumiit totum campum et elegit et amavit, et coepit fides crescere
ibi.

13 Adpropinquavit autem pascha in diebus illis, quod pasca primum Deo
in nostra Aegipto huius insolae velut quondam in Gessen* celebr-
atum est. Et inierunt* consilium ubi hoc primum pasca in gentibus ad
quas missit illos Deus celebrarent, multisque super hac re consiliis
iectis, postremo inspirato divinitus sancto Patricio vissum est hanc
magnam Domini sollempnitatem quasi caput omnium sollempnitatum
in campo maximo, ubi erat regnum maximum nationum harum †quod
erat omnis gentilitatis et idolatriae caput, celebrari,†* ut hic invictus
cuneus in caput totius idolatriae, ne possit ulterius adversus Christi
fidem insurgere, sub malleo fortis operis cum fide iuncti sancti
Patricii et suorum manibus primus inlideretur; et sic factum est.

14 Elevata igitur navis ad mare, et dimisso in fide plena et pace bono illo
viro Dichu, migrantes de campo Iniss dexteraque manu demittentes
omnia ad plenitudinem ministerii quae erant ante non incongrue leva,
in portum Hostii Colpdi bene et prospere delati sunt. Relictaque ibi
navi, pedistri itenere venierunt in praedictum maximum campum,
donec postremo ad vesperum pervenierunt ad Ferti virorum Feec,
quam, ut fabulae ferunt, foderunt viri, id est servi, Feecol Ferchertni,
qui fuerat unus e novim magis prophetis Bregg. Fixoque ibi tentorio,
debeta pascae vota sacrificiumque laudis cum omni devotione sanctus
Patricius cum suis Deo altissimo secundum profetae vocem reddidit.

15 Contigit vero in illo anno idolatriae sollempnitatem, quam gentiles
incantationibus multis et magicis inventionibus nonnullisque aliis
idolatriae superstitionibus, congregatis etiam regibus, satrapis, ducibus,

principibus et optimatibus populi, insuper et magis, incantatoribus,
auruspicibus et omnis artis omnisque doli* inventoribus doctoribusve
vocatis ad Loigaireum velut quondam ad Nabcodonossor regem, in
Temoria, istorum Babylone, exercere consuerant, eadem nocte qua
sanctus Patricius pasca, illi illam adorarent exercerentque festivitatem
gentilem. Erat quoque quidam mos apud illos, per edictum omnibus
intimatus, ut quicumque in cunctis regionibus sive procul sive iuxta in
illa nocte incendisset ignem antequam in domu regia, id est in palatio
Temoriae, succenderetur, periret anima eius de populo suo.

Sanctus ergo Patricius, sanctum pasca celebrans, incendit divinum
ignem valde lucidum et benedictum, qui in nocte reffulgens a cunctis
pene per planitiem campi habitantibus vissus est. Accidit ergo ut a
Temoria videretur, vissoque eo conspexerunt omnes et mirati sunt.
Convocatisque senioribus et maioribus natu et magis, dixit eis rex:
'Quid est hoc? Quis est qui hoc nefas ausus est facere in regno meo?
Pereat ille morte.' Et respondentibus omnibus senioribus et maioribus
natu* regi nesciisse illum qui hoc fecerit, magi responderunt: 'Rex, in
aeternum vive. Hic ignis quem videmus quique in hac nocte accensus
est antequam succenderetur in domu tua, id est in palatio Temoriae,
nissi extinctus fuerit in nocte hac qua accensus est, nunquam extin-
guetur in aeternum; insuper et omnes ignes nostrae consuitudinis
supergradietur; et ille qui incendit et regnum superveniens a quo
incensus est in hac nocte superabit nos omnes et te, et omnes homines
regni tui seducet et cadent ei omnia regna, et ipsum implebit omnia
et regnabit in saecula saeculorum.'

16 His ergo auditis turbatus est rex Loiguire valde, ut olim Erodis, et
omnis civitas Temoria cum eo. Et respondens dixit: 'Non sic erit; sed
nunc nos ibimus ut videamus exitum rei, et retinebimus et occidemus
facientes tantum nefas in nostrum regnum.' Iunctis igitur ter novem*
curribus secundum deorum traditionem et assumptis his duobus magis
ad conflictionem prae omnibus optimis, id est Lucetmael et Lochru,
in fine noctis illius perrexit Loiguire de Temoria ad Ferti virorum
Feec, hominum et equorum facies secundum congruum illis sensum
ad levam vertentes.

Euntibus autem illis, dixerunt magi regi: 'Rex, nec tu ibis ad locum
in quo ignis est incensus, ne forte tu postea adoraveris illum qui
incendit; sed eris foris iuxta, et vocabitur ad te ille ut te adoraverit et
tu ipse dominatus fueris, et sermocinabimur ad invicem nos et ille in
conspectu tuo, rex, et probabis nos sic.' Et respondens rex ait: 'Bonum
consilium invenistis; sic faciam ut locuti fuistis.' Et pervenierunt ad

praefinitum locum, discendentibusque illis de curribus suis et equis, non intraverunt in circuitum loci incensi, sed sederunt iuxta.

17   Et vocatus est sanctus Patricius ad regem extra locum incensi. Dixeruntque magi ad suos: 'Nec surgemus nos in adventu istius; nam quicunque surrexerit ad adventum istius credet ei postea et adorabit eum.' Surgens denique sanctus Patricius et videns multos currus et equos eorum, huncque psalmistae versiculum non incongrue in labiis et in corde decantans: 'Hii in curribus et hii in equis, nos autem in nomine Dei nostri ambulabimus;' venit ad illos. Illi non surrexerunt in adventu eius; sed unus tantum a Domino adiutus, qui noluit oboedire dictis magorum, hoc est Ercc filius Dego, cuius nunc reliquiae adorantur in illa civitate quae vocatur Slane, surrexit; et benedixit eum Patricius, et credidit Deo aeterno.

Incipientibusque illis sermocinari ad invicem, alter magus, nomine Lochru, procax erat in conspectu sancti, audens detrachere fidei catholicae tumulentis verbis. Hunc autem intuens turvo oculo talia promentem sanctus Patricius, ut quondam Petrus de Simone, cum quadam potentia et magno clamore confidenter ad Dominum dixit: 'Domine, qui omnia potés et in tua potestate consistunt, quique me missisti huc, hic impius qui blasfemat nomen tuum elevetur nunc foras et cito moriatur.' Et his dictis, elivatus est in aethera magus et iterum dimissus foras desuper, verso ad lapidem cerebro, comminutus et mortuus fuerat coram eis; et timuerunt gentiles.

18   Iratusque cum suis rex Patricio super hoc, voluit eum occidere et dixit: 'Iniecite manus in istum perdentem nos.' Tunc videns gentiles impios inruituros in eum, sanctus Patricius surrexit claraque voce dixit: 'Exsurgat Deus et dissipentur inimici eius, et fugiant qui oderunt eum a facie eius.' Et statim inruerunt tenebrae et commotio quaedam horribilis, et expugnaverunt impii semetipsos alter adversus alterum insurgens; et terrae motus magnus factus est, et collocavit axes curruum eorum et agebat eos cum vi, et praecipitaverunt se currus et equi per planitiem campi, donec ad extremum pauci ex eis semivivi evasserunt ad montem Monduirn. Et prostrati sunt ab hac plaga coram rege et suis senioribus* ad maledictum Patricii septem septies viri, donec ipse remanserat †cum septem tantum hominibus, ipse et uxor eius et duos reges et alii ex sociis quattuor†*. Et timuerunt valde.

Veniensque regina ad Patricium dixit ei: 'Homo iuste et potens, ne perdas regem; veniens enim rex genua flectet et adorabit Dominum tuum.' Et venit rex timore coactus et flexit genua coram sancto et

finxit se adorare quem nolebat. Et postquam separaverunt ad invicem, paululum gradiens vocavit rex sanctum Patricium simulato verbo,
volens interficere eum quo modo. Sciens autem Patricius cogitationes
regis pessimi, benedictis in nomine Iesu Christi sociis suis octo
viris cum puero, venit ad regem. Enumerat eos rex venientes, statim-
que nusquam comparuerunt ab oculis regis dempti;* sed viderunt
gentiles octo tantum cervos cum hynulo euntes quasi ad dissertum.
Et rex Loiguire mestus, timidus et ignominiossus cum paucis evadent-
ibus ad Temoriam reversus est deluculo.

19   Sequenti vero die, hoc est in die pascae, recumbentibus regibus et
     principibus et magis apud Loiguire (festus enim dies maximus apud
     eos erat), manducantibus illis et bibentibus vinum in palatio Temoriae
     sermocinantibusque aliis et aliis cogitantibus de his quae facta fuerant,
     sanctus Patricius cum quinque tantum viris,* ut contenderet et verbum
     faceret de fide sancta in Temoria coram omnibus nationibus, hostiis
     clausis, secundum id quod de Christo legitur, venit.

     Adveniente ergo eo in caenacolum Temoriae nemo de omnibus ad
     adventum eius surrexit praeter unum tantum, id est Dubthoch Maccu
     Lugil, poetam optimum, apud quem tunc temporis ibi erat quidam
     adoliscens poeta, nomine Feec, qui postea   mirabilis episcopus fuit,
     cuius reliquiae adorantur *hi* Sleibti. Hic, ut dixi, Dubthach solus ex
     gentibus in honorem sancti Patricii surrexit; et benedixit ei sanctus,
     crediditque primus in illa die Deo, et repputatum est ei ad iustitiam.
     Visso itaque Patricio, vocatus est a gentibus ad vescendum, ut
     probarent eum in venturis rebus. Ille autem, sciens quae ventura essent,
     non reffellit vesci.

20   Caenantibus autem omnibus, ille magus Lucet mail, qui fuerat in
     nocturna conflictione, etiam in illa die solicitus est extincto consocio
     suo confligere adversus sanctum Patricium; et ut initium causae
     haberet, intuentibus aliis inmissit aliquid ex vasse suo in poculum
     Patricii, ut probaret quid faceret. Vidensque sanctus Patricius hoc
     probationis genus, videntibus cunctis benedixit poculum suum, et
     versus est liquor in modum gelu; et conversso vasse cecidit gutta illa
     tantum quam inmisserat magus. Et iterum benedixit poculum;
     conversus est liquor in naturam, et mirati sunt omnes.

     Et post paululum ait magus: 'Faciamus signa in hoc campo maximo.'
     Respondensque Patricius ait: 'Quae?' Et dixit magus: 'Inducamus
     nivem super terram.' Et ait Patricius:* 'Nolo contraria voluntati Dei
     inducere.' Et dixit magus: 'Ego inducam videntibus cunctis.' Tunc
     incantationes magicas exorsus induxit nivem super totum campum

pertinguentem *ferenn*; et viderunt omnes et mirati sunt. Et ait sanctus:
'Ecce videmus hoc; depone nunc.' Et dixit: 'Ante istam horam cras
non possum deponere.' Et ait sanctus: 'Potes malum et non bonum
facere. Non sic ego.' Tunc benedicens per totum circuitum campum,
dicto citius absque ulla pluia aut nebulis aut vento evanuit nix. Et
clamaverunt turbae et mirati sunt et compuncti sunt corde.*

Et paulo post invocatis demonibus induxit magus densissimas
tenebras super terram in signum; et mormuraverunt omnes. Et ait
sanctus: 'Expelle tenebras.' At ille similiter non poterat. Sanctus
autem orans benedixit, et reppente expulsae sunt tenebrae et refulsit
sol. Et exclamaverunt omnes et gratias egerunt. His autem omnibus
in conspectu regis inter magum Patriciumque gestis, ait rex ad illos:
'Libros vestros in aquam mittite, et illum cuius libri inlessi evasserunt
adorabimus.' Respondit Patricius: 'Faciam ego.' Et dixit magus: "Nolo
ego ad iudicium aquae venire cum isto; aquam enim Deum habet.'
(Certe audivit babtisma per aquam a Patricio datum). Et respondens
rex ait: 'Permitte per ignem.' Et ait Patricius: 'Prumptus sum.' At
magus nolens dixit: 'Hic homo versa vice in alternos annos nunc
aquam, nunc ignem deum veneratur.' Et ait sanctus: 'Non sic. Sed tu
ipse ibis, et unus ex meis pueris ibit tecum in separatam et conclaussam
domum, et meum erga te et tuum erga meum puerum* erit vestim-
entum, et sic simul incendemini.'

Et hoc consilium insedit, et aedificata est eis domus cuius dimedium
ex materia viridi et alterum dimedium ex arida facta est. Et missus est
magus in illam domum in partem eius viridem cum casula Patricii erga
eum,* et unus e pueris sancti Patricii, Bineus nomine, cum veste
magica in partem domus aridam.* Conclussa itaque extrinsecus
domus coram omni turba incensa est. Et factum est in illa hora, orante
Patricio, ut consumeret flamma ignis magum cum demedia domu viridi,
permanente cassula sancti Patricii tantum intacta, quam ignis non
tetigit. Felix autem Benineus e contrario cum demedia domu arida;
secundum quod de tribus pueris dictum est, non tetigit eum ignis
neque contristatus est nec quicquam molesti intulit; cassula tantum
magi, quae erga eum fuerat, non sine Dei nutu exusta.

Et iratus est valde rex adversus Patricium de morte magi sui, et
inruit poenc in eum volens occidere; sed prohibuit illum Deus. Ad
precem enim Patricii et ad vocem eius discendit ira Dei in populum
inpium, et perierunt multi ex eis. Et ait sanctus Patricius regi: 'Nisi
nunc credideris, cito morieris, quia descendet* ira Dei in verticem
tuum.' Et timuit rex vehementer, et commotum est cor eius, et omnis

civitas cum eo.

21 Congregatis igitur senioribus et omni senatu suo, dixit eis rex Loiguire: 'Melius est credere me quam mori.' Initoque consilio, ex suorum praecepto credidit in illa die et convertit ad Dominum Deum aeternum; et ibi crediderunt multi alii. Et ait sanctus Patricius ad regem: 'Quia resististi doctrinae meae et fuisti scandalum mihi, licet prolonguentur dies regni tui, nullus tamen erit ex semine tuo rex in aeternum post te.'

22 Sanctus autem Patricius, secundum praeceptum Domini Iesu iens et docens omnes* gentes babtitxansque eas in nomine Patris et Filii et Spiritus sancti, profectus a Temoria praedicavit Domino cooperante et sermonem confirmante sequentibus signis.

The Brussels and Vienna MSS (B and C) begin book 2 after this point.

23 Erat quidam homo in regionibus Ulothorum Patricii tempore, Macuil Maccugreccae nomine*, et erat hic homo valde impius, saevus tyrannus, ut Cyclops nominaretur. Cogitationibus pravus, verbis intemperatus, factis malignus, spiritu amarus, animo iracondus, corpore scelestus, mente crudelis, vita gentilis, conscientia immanis,* in tantum vergens impietatis in profundum ita ut die quadam in montosso, aspero altoque sedens loco Hindruim Moccuechach, ubi ille tyrannidem cotidie exercebat signa sumens nequissima crudelitatis et transeuntes hospites crudeli scelere interficiens, sanctum quoque Patricium claro fidei lumine radiantem et miro quodam caelestis gloriae deademate fulgentem, videns eum inconcussa doctrinae fiducia per congruum viae iter ambulantem, interficere cogitaret, dicens satilitibus suis: 'Ecce, seductor ille et perversor hominum venit, cui mos facere praestigias ut decipiat homines multosque seducat. Eamus ergo et temptemus eum, et sciemus si habet potentiam aliquam ille Deus in quo se gloriatur.'

Temptaveruntque virum sanctum in hoc modo*; posuerunt unum ex semetipsis sanum in medio eorum sub sago iacentem infirmitatemque mortis simulantem, ut probarent sanctum in huiusquemodi fallaci re, sanctum seductorem, virtutes praestigias, et orationes veneficia vel

incantationes nominantes. Adveniente sancto Patricio cum discipulis
suis, gentiles dixerunt ei: 'Ecce, unus ex nobis nunc infirmatus est.
Accede itaque ⸗t canta super eum aliquas incantationes sectae tuae,
si forte sanari possit.' Sanctus Patricius, sciens omnes dolos et fallacias
eorum, constanter et intripide ait: 'Nec mirum si infirmus fuisset.' Et
revelantes socii eius faciem insimulantis infirmitatem, viderunt eum
iam mortuum. At illi obstupescentes ammirantesque tale miraculum,
dixerunt intra se gementes:* 'Vere hic homo Dei est; male fecimus
temptantes eum.'

Sanctus vero Patricius conversus ad Maccuil ait: 'Quare temptare me
voluisti?' Respondensque ille tyrannus crudelis ait: 'Poeniteat me
facti huius, et quodcumque praeciperis mihi faciam, et trado me nunc
in potentiam Dei tui excelsi quem praedicas.' Et ait sanctus: 'Crede
ergo in Deo meo Domino Iesu, et confitere peccata tua et babtizare
in nomine Patris et Filii et Spiritus sancti.' Et conversus in illa hora
credidit Deo aeterno, babtitzatusque est. Insuper et haec* addidit
Maccuil dicens: 'Confiteor tibi, sancte domine mi Patrici, quod
proposui te interficere. Iudica ergo quantum debuerit pro tanto ac
tali cremine.'

Et ait Patricius: 'Non possum iudicare, sed Deus iudicabit. Tu tamen
egredire nunc inermis ad mare, et transi velociter de regione hac
Hibernensi, nihil tollens tecum de tua substantia praeter vile et parvum
indumentum quo possit corpus tuum contegi, nihil gustans nihilque
bibens de fructu insolae huius, habens insigne peccati tui in capite tuo;
et postquam pervenias ad mare, conliga pedes tuos conpede ferreo, et
proiece clavim eius in mari, et mitte te in navim unius pellis absque
gubernaculo et absque remo, et quocumque te duxerit ventus et mare
esto paratus, et terram in quamcumque defferat te divina providentia,
inhabita et exerce ibi divina mandata.' Dixitque Maccuill: 'Sic faciam
ut dixisti. De viro autem mortuo quid faciemus?' Et ait Patricius:
'Vivet et exsurget sine dolore.' Et suscitavit eum Patricius in illa hora,
et revixit sanus.

Et migravit inde Maccuil tam cito ad mare dexterum campi Inis,
habeta fiducia inconcussa fidei, collegavitque se in litore ieciens clavim
in mare secundum quod praeceptum est ei, et ascendit mare in
navicula. Et inspiravit illi ventus aquilo et sustulit eum ad meridiem
iecitque eum in insolam, Evoniam nomine. Invenitque ibi duos viros
valde mirabiles, in fide et doctrina fulgentes, qui primi docuerunt
verbum Dei et babtismum in Evonia, et conversi sunt homines insolae
in doctrina eorum ad fidem catholicam, quorum nomina sunt

Conindri et Rumili. Hii vero videntes virum unius habitus mirati sunt et miserti sunt illius, elivaveruntque de mari suscipientes cum gaudio. Ille igitur, ubi inventi sunt spiritales patres in regione a Deo sibi credita, ad regulam eorum corpus et animam exercuit, et totum vitae tempus exegit apud istos duos sanctos episcopos, usque dum successor eorum in episcopatu effectus est. Hic est Maccuil *dimane* episcopus et antestes Arddae Huimnonn.

24 Alia vero vice sanctus requiescens Patricius in die dominica supra mare iuxta salsuginem quae est ad aquilonalem plagam a Collo Bovis distans non magno viae* spatio, audivit sonum intemperatum gentilium in die dominica laborantium, facientium *rathi,* vocatisque illis prohibuit eos Patricius ne laborarent in dominico die. At illi non consentiebant verbis sancti; quin immo inridentes deludebant eum. Et ait sanctus Patricius: 'Mudebroth, quamvis laboraveritis, nec tamen proficiat.' Quod tamen completum est. In sequenti enim nocte ventus magnus adveniens turbavit mare, et omne opus gentilium destruxit tempestas, iuxta verbum sancti.

25 Fuit quidam homo dives et honorabilis in regionibus Orientalium cui nomen erat Daire. Hunc autem rogavit Patricius ut aliquem locum ad exercendam relegionem daret ei. Dixitque dives ad sanctum: 'Quem locum petis?' 'Peto,' inquit sanctus, 'ut illam altitudinem terrae quae nominatur Dorsum Salicis dones mihi, et construam ibi locum.' At ille noluit sancto terram illam dare altam, sed dedit illi locum alium in inferiori terra, ubi nunc est *Fertae* Martyrum iuxta Ardd machae, et habitavit ibi sanctus Patricius cum suis.

Post vero aliquod tempus venit eques † *doiri* † Dairi ducens equum suum mirabilem,* ut pasceretur in herbosso loco Christianorum. Et offendit Patricium talis dilatio equi in locum suum, et ait: 'Stulte fecit Daire bruta mittens animalia turbare locum parvum quem dedit Deo.' At vero eques tanquam sordus non audiebat et sicut mutus non aperiens os suum nihil loquebatur, sed dimisso ibi equo nocte illa exivit. Crastino autem die mane veniens eques vissitare equum suum, invenit eum iam mortuum. Domique reversus tristis ait ad dominum suum: 'Ecce, Christianus ille occidit equum tuum. Offendit enim illum turbatio loci sui.' Et dixit Daire: 'Occidatur et ille; nunc ite et interficite eum.'

Euntibus autem illis foras, dictu citius inruit mors super Daire. Et ait uxor eius: 'Causa Christiani est haec mors.* Eat quis cito, et portentur nobis beneficia eius, et salvus eris; et prohibeantur* et revocentur qui

exierunt occidere eum.' Exieruntque duo viri ad Christianum qui
dixerunt ei, celantes quod factum est: 'Et ecce, infirmatus est Daire;
portetur illi aliquid a te, si forte sanari possit.' Sanctus autem
Patricius, sciens quae facta sunt, dixit: 'Nimirum.' Benedixitque
aquam et dedit dicens: 'Ite, aspergite equum vestrum ex aqua ista, et
portate illam vobiscum.' Et fecerunt sic, et revixit equus; et
portaverunt secum, sanatusque est Daire asparsione aquae sanctae.

Et venit Daire post haec ut honoraret sanctum Patricium, portans
secum aeneum mirabilem transmarinum metritas ternas capientem.
Dixitque Daire ad sanctum: 'Ecce hic aeneus sit tecum.' Et ait
sanctus Patricius: 'Grazacham.' Reversusque Daire ad domum suam
dixit: 'Stultus homo est qui nihil boni dixit praeter grazacham pro
aeneo mirabili metritarum trium.' Additque Daire dicens servis suis:
'Ite, reportate nobis aeneum nostrum.' Exierunt et dixerunt Patricio:
'Portabimus aeneum.' Nihilominus et illa vice sanctus Patricius dixit:
'Gratzacham, portate;' et portaverunt. Interrogavitque Daire socios
suos dicens: 'Quid dixit Christianus quando reportastis aeneum?' At
illi responderunt: 'Grazacham dixit et ille.' Daire respondens dixit:
'Gratzacham in dato, grazacham in ablato; eius dictum tam bonum
est — cum grazacham illis portabitur illi rursum aeneus suus.' Et venit
Daire ipsemet illa vice et portavit aeneum ad Patricium, dicens ei:
'Fiat tecum aeneus tuus. Constans enim et incommotabilis homo es.
Insuper et partem illam agri quam ollim petisti do tibi nunc quantum
habeo, et inhabita ibi.' Et illa est civitas quae nunc Arddmachae
nominatur.

Et exierunt ambo, sanctus Patricius et Daire, ut considerarent mirabile
oblationis et beneplacitum munus, et ascenderunt illam altitudinem
terrae, invenieruntque cervam cum vitulo suo parvo iacente in loco in
quo nunc altare est sinistralis aeclessiae in Ardd mache. Et voluerunt
comites Patricii tenere vitulum et occidere, sed noluit sanctus neque
permissit; quin potius ipsemet sanctus tenuit vitulum portans eum in
humeris suis. Et secuta illum cerva velut mitissima mansuetissimaque*
ovis usquedum dimisserat vitulum in altero saltu sito* ad aquilonalem
plagam Airdd mache, ubi usque hodie signa quaedam virtutis eius
manentia periti dicunt.

26   Virum aliquem valde durum et tam avarum in campo Inis habitantem
      in tantum stultitiae avaritiaeque incurrisse cremen periti ferunt, ut
      duos boves carrum* Patricii vechentes, alio die post sanctum laborem
      in pastu agili sui requiescentibus pascentibusque se bobus, violenter
      inconstanter praesente sancto Patricio vanus ille homo per vim coegit.

Cui irascens sanctus Patricius cum maledictione dixit: '*Mudebrod*, male fecisti. Nusquam proficiat tibi ager hic tuus neque semini tuo in aeternum; iam inutilis erit.' Et factum est sic. Inundatio etenim maris tam habunda eodem veniens die circumluit et operuit totum agrum, et positus* est iuxta profetae verbum terra fructifera in salsuginem a malitia inhabitantis in ea. Arenossa ergo et infructuossa haec a die qua maledixit eam sanctus Patricius usque in hodiernum diem.

27 [Itaque, volente Domino, Patricii ut ita dicam totius Hiberniae episcopi doctorisque egregii de virtutibus pauca pluribus ennarrare conabor.] * Quodam igitur tempore, cum tota Britannia incredulitatis algore rigesceret, cuiusdam regis egregia filia, cui nomen erat Monesan, Spiritus sancti repleta auxilio, cum quidam eius expeteret amplexus coniugalis, non adquievit* ⟨neque⟩ cum aquarum multis irrigata esset undis ad id quod nolebat et deterius erat compelli potuit. Nam illa cum inter verbera et aquarum irrigationes solita esset interrogare* matrem et nutricem utrum compertum haberent* rotae factorem qua totus illuminatur mundus, et cum responsum acciperet per quod compertum haberet solis factorem esse eum cui caelum sedes est, cum acta esset frequenter ut coniugali vinculo copularetur, luculentissimo Spiritus sancti ⟨consilio⟩* illustrata ⟨dicebat⟩*: 'Nequaquam itaque hoc faciam.' Quaerebat namque per naturam totius creaturae factorem, in hoc patriarchae Abraham secuta exemplum.

Parentes eius inito consilio a Deo sibi tributo,* audito Patricio viro ab aeterno Deo visitari* septimo semper die, Scoticas* partes † cum filia ⟨petentes⟩ pulsaverunt Patricium, quem tanto labore quesitum repererunt.†* Qui illos novicos percunctari coepit. Tunc illi viatores clamare ceperunt et dicere: 'Cupidissimae filiae videndi Deum causa coacti ad te venire facti sumus.' Tunc ille repletus Spiritu sancto elevavit vocem suam et dixit ad eam: 'Si in Deum credis?' Et ait: 'Credo.' Tunc sacro Spiritu et aquae lavacro eam lavit. Nec mora; postea solo prostrata spiritum in manus angelorum tradidit. Ubi moritur ibi et adunatur. Tunc Patricius prophetavit quod post annos viginti corpus illius ad propinquam cellulam de illo loco tolleretur omni honore; quod postea ita factum est. Cuius transmarinae reliquiae ibi adorantur usque hodie.

28 Dominici et apostolici Patricii, cuius mentionem facimus, quoddam miraculum mirifice gestum, quod ei in carne adhuc stanti* et Stephano poene tantum* contigisse legitur, brevi retexam relatu. Quodam autem* tempore, cum orationis causa ad locum solitum per nocturna spacia procederet, consueta caeli vidit miracula, suumque carissimum

ac fidelem probare volens sanctum puerum, dixit: 'O fili mi, dic
michi, quaeso, si sentis ea quae ego sentio.' Tunc parvulus, nomine
Benignus, incunctanter dixit: 'Iam mihi cognita ea quae sentis. Nam
video caelum apertum et Filium Dei et angelos eius.' Tunc Patricius
dixit: 'Iam te meum successorem dignum esse sentio.' Nec mora,
gradu concito ad suetum locum orationis pervenere.* His ergo
orantibus* in medio fluminis alveo, parvulus dixit: 'Iam algorem
aquaticum sustinere non possum.' Nam ei aqua nimis erat frigida. Tunc
dixit ei Patricius ut de superiori ⟨loco⟩* ad inferiorem descenderet.
Nichilominus ibi diu* perstare ⟨non⟩* potuit. Nam se aquam
calidam sensisse testabatur. Tunc ille non sustinens in eo loco diu
stare terram ascendit.

29   Quoddam mirabile gestum Patricii non transibo silentio. Huic
     nuntiatum est nequissimum opus cuiusdam regis Britannici nomine
     Corictic, infausti crudelisque tyranni. Hic namque erat maximus
     persecutor interfectorque Christianorum. Patricius autem per epist-
     olam ad viam veritatis revocare temptavit; cuius salutaria deridebat
     monita. Cum autem ista* nuntiarentur Patricio, oravit Dominum et
     dixit: 'Deus, si fieri potest, expelle hunc perfidum de presenti seculo-
     que futuro.' Non grande postea tempus effluxerat,* et ⟨Corictic⟩*
     musicam artem audivit a quodam cantari* quod ⟨cito⟩* de solio
     regali transiret. Omnesque karissimi eius viri in hanc proruperunt
     vocem. Tunc ille, cum esset in medio foro, ilico vulpeculae* miser-
     abiliter arepta forma, profectus in suorum presentia, ex illo die
     illaque hora velut fluxus aquae transiens nusquam conparuit.

TEXTUAL NOTES

Manuscripts

A   Dublin, Trinity College, MS. 52 (Armagh, A.D. 807)
B   Brussels, Bibliothèque royale, MS. 64 (11th cent.)
C   Vienna, Oesterreichische Nationalbibliothek, ser. nov. 3642 (late 8th cent.)
N   Novara, Biblioteca capitolare, MS. 77 (13th cent.)

Other lives of St. Patrick

P (Probus); V2 (Vita secunda); V3 (Vita tertia); V4 (Vita quarta) — all edited by Ludwig Bieler, *Four Latin Lives of St. Patrick* (Dublin, 1971)

Previous editors

Gwynn   John Gwynn (ed.), *Liber Ardmachanus* (Dublin, 1913)
Hogan   E. Hogan, *Analecta Bollandiana* 1 (1882) 531-85

Pref; Coguitosi *Hogan*: cognito si *A*

1.   ven tre *B*: Nemthor *V2V3V4*
     sexennium . . . ⟨in ea captivitate exegit⟩ *Hogan* (*cf. V2V4P*):
       sexennem *B*
     reddens ⟨quae Dei . . . Caesari⟩ *Hogan* (*cf. P*): rediens *B*
     deserto tiranno gentilique homine *B*: deserto itaque rege terreno *N*
     in comitatu sancti spiritus ex praecepto divino *Bieler*: in comitatu
       sancto excepto divino *B*: praecepito enim divino admonitus,
       spiritu sancto comitatus *N*
5.   ⟨occurrens in mensuram aetatis⟩ *P*: et cetera usque *B*
     itaque *B*
     sapienciam divinam *N*: sapiens iam divina *B*
6.   accepto itinere per Gallicas *B*: ceptoque per Gallias itinere *N*
     ⟨Galliarum paene omnium⟩ summum dominum *Bury* (*cf. V2V4P*):
       summum donum *B*
     virgo corpore et spiritu *V3* (*cf. P*): vigore *B*
7.   peractis *NV4*: factisque *B*
     antiquitus amicus valde fidelis *N*: antiquus valde fidelis *B*
8.   certi etenim erant *CNV2*: certe enim erat *A*: ceteri enim erant *B*
     Deus *om. A*
     Britonum *A V3*: Pictorum *CBNPV2V4*

functus est *CB*: factus *A*

9.   illi *CBP*: ibi *A*: sibi *V2*: ei *V4*

10.   pene totius *Bury*: huius pene *A*

de *om.A*

reges occisurum *CBNV2V4*: *om.A*

propter linguae idioma *CB*: pro linguae idiomo *A*

curvicipite *CN*: curvi capite *A*: curvo capite *B*: et sua domu
    White: ex sua (ex ea sua *C*) domu *ACBN*: capite perforata *B*:
    capita perforata *C*: capite perforato *AN*

11.   in *CB*: *om.A*

12.   iterum *AB*: iterum reversum *V3*: iturum *Hogan*: venire *N*
    (*cf. PV2V4*)

13.   Gessen *Gwynn.* (*cf. V2P*): Genesseon *A*: Genesim *B*

inierunt *NPV2V4*: ininierunt *B*: invenierunt *A*

quod erat omnis gentilitatis et idolatriae ne possit ulterius liberari
    A: ubi maxime caput gentilitatis et idolatriae praestiterat
    censuit celebrari *V2V4* (*cf. P*): quod erat omnis gentilitatis et
    idolatriae caput draconis confringeret a servis Dei excelsi
    celebrari *B*

15.   doli *Hogan*: doni *A*

et magis . . . maioribus natu *om.A*

16.   ergo ter novam *P*: igitur ternis novies *V2V4*: ergo . . . ternis nonies
    B: ternis nonisque *N*

18.   ac suis senioribus *B*: ex suis sermonibus *A*

remanserat tantum hominibus ipse et uxor eius et alii ex Scotis
    duo *A*: remanserat quattuor tantum ipse et uxor eius et alii ex sociis
    duo *B* (*cf. V2*): ipse rex cum septem tantum hominibus remansit
    illaesus, uxore videlicet sua et duobus regibus nec non et
    quattuor viris *P*

dempti *BNV2*: *om.A*

19.   cum *om.AB*: cum quinque viris *V2*: cum duobus tantum viris *P*:
    quinque viris comitantibus *V4*

20.   Patricius *CBV2V3V4*: pater *A*

mirati sunt et compuncti sunt corde *V3*: mirata est valde plebs et
    compuncta est corde *C* (*cf.NV4*): mirati sunt corde *AP*: mirate
    sunt valde *B*

meum puerum *PV2*: me *A*

cum casula Patricii erga eum *C* (*cf. P*): *om.AB*

aridam *CPV3*: *om.A*: in parte domus aridae *B*

ira Dei in populum . . . quia descendet *om.A*

22.   iens et docens omnes *om.A*

23.   nomine *BN* (*cf. PV3*): *om.A*

immanis *BN*: inanis *A*

hoc modo *P*: hoc homo *B*: hoc mundo temptaverunt et *A*

gementes *BNP*: gentes *A* (*cf. V3*)

haec *Gwynn* (et haec audivit Macuil *B*): non *A*

24. viae *B*: vice *A*
25. equum suum mirabilem *Gwynn* (cum equo suo mirabili *V3*):
    equum suum miraculum *A*: equum suum et ait stulte mirabile *B*
    haec mors *BP*: haec *A*: hoc *N*
    prohibeantur *Gwynn*: prohibeant *B*: prohibentur *A*
    mitissima ac mansuetissima *P*: mitissima *NV3V4*: amantissimaque *A*
    situm *A*
26. carrarum *A*
    positus *A*: posita *NP*
27. (this sentence marks the beginning of book 2 in *B*; and follows
    there immediately after ch. 22)
    adquieum *B*
    interrogare *Hogan*: interrogabat *B*
    utrum compertum haberent *N*: uti compertum haberet *B*
    illustrata consilio *N*
    ⟨dicebat⟩ *Hogan*
    iusti tributo *B*: sibi tradito *P*
    visitato *B*
    Scoticas *Hogan*: sconas *B*
    cum filia pulsavere Patricium quem tanto labore quesitum reperire
        B: cum filia petiverunt quaerentes Patricium quem tanto labore
        quesitum reperire meruerunt *Hogan*
28. quod ei in carne adhuc stanti *Hogan*: in carne adhuc quod ei *B*
    tantum *Hogan* (tantum fere esse commune *N*): totum *B*
    ante *B*: enim *N*
    pervenere *Hogan*: pervenire *B*
    his orationibus *B*: illis ergo orantibus *N*: his ergo in oratione
        constitutis *P*
    loco *P* (*cf. N*): om.*B*
    diu *P*: duo *B*
    non *P* (*cf. N*): om.*B*
29. ista *Hogan*: ita *B*
    effluxerat *Hogan*: effluxuat *B*
    ⟨Corictic⟩ *e.g.*: praefatus ille tyrannus *P*
    cantari *N*: cantare *B*: praecantari *P*
    cito *P*: om.*BN*
    vulpeculae *PNV3*: vel ficuli *B*

TRANSLATION

Preface

Many, my lord Aed, have attempted to organise this particular
narrative in accordance with the tradition handed down to them by
their fathers and by those who have been storytellers from the
beginning, but because of the grave difficulties involved in recounting
it and of differing opinions and numerous persons' numerous con-
jectures they have never succeeded in reaching the one sure path of
historical fact; and so, if I am not mistaken, as our people's saying
here goes, just as boys are brought into the meeting-place, so I have
brought the child's rowing-boat of my poor intellect onto this deep
and dangerous ocean of hagiography, with the waves surging in
wildly swirling walls of water, among whirlpools and jagged rocks
in uncharted seas - an ocean never yet attempted or embarked on
by any barque except only that of my father Cogitosus. However, to
avoid giving the impression that I am exaggerating, I shall, with some
reluctance, set about expounding this small and piece-meal selection
from St. Patrick's numerous acts. I have little talent, dubious
authorities, and am subject to lapses of memory; I have only feeble
insight and a poor style; but I am prompted by dutiful and loving
affection and am obedient to the command of your holiness and
dignity.

29.   St. Patrick's conflict with Coroticus, king of Ail.

These few items concerning St. Patrick's experience and miraculous
powers were written down by Muirchu maccu Machtheni under the
direction of Aed, bishop of the town of Sletty.

1   Patrick, who was also called Sochet, was of British nationality,
born in Britain, the son of the deacon Calpurnius, whose father,
as Patrick himself says, was the priest Potitus, who came from the
town of Bannavem Taburniae, not far from our sea; we have discovered
for certain and beyond any doubt that this township is Ventre; and the
mother who bore him was named Concessa.
        At the age of sixteen the boy, with others, was captured and brought
to this island of barbarians and was kept as a slave in the household of
a certain cruel pagan king. He spent six years in captivity, in accordance
with the Jewish custom, in fear and trembling before God, as the
psalmist says (*Psalms 54, 6*), and in many vigils and prayers. He
used to pray a hundred times a day and a hundred times a night,
gladly giving to God what is due to God and to Caesar what is due
to Caesar and beginning to fear God and to love the Lord Almighty;
for up to that time he had no knowledge of the true God, but at this
point the Spirit became fervent within him.
        After many hardships there, after enduring hunger and thirst, cold
and nakedness, after pasturing flocks, after visits from Victoricus, an angel
sent to him by God, after great miracles known to almost everyone,
after divine prophecies (of which I shall give just one or two examples:
'You do well to fast, since you will soon be going to your home country,'
and again: 'See, your ship is ready,' though it was not near at hand but
was perhaps two hundred miles away, where he had never been to)
-after all these experiences, as we have said, which can hardly be counted
by anyone, in the twenty-third year of his life he left the earthly, pagan
king and his works, received the heavenly, eternal God and now sailed
for Britain by God's command and accompanied by the Holy Spirit in
the ship which lay ready for him; with him were barbarian strangers
and pagans who worshipped many false gods.

2   So for three days and as many nights he was tossed at sea with
the ungodly, like Jonah, and after that for the space of twenty-eight
days he toiled through the wilderness, just as Moses did, though
with a different significance; as the pagans almost collapsed from hunger
and thirst, they grumbled, like the Jews. He was urged by the captain
and put under pressure and asked to pray to his God for them that
they should not perish; he was prevailed upon by mortal men; he took
pity on the band, he was troubled in spirit, was deservedly crowned,

was magnified by God - he supplied them with an abundance of food from the herd of pigs sent him by God, just as Moses fed the Children of Israel from the flock of quails with God's help. There was also wild honey to succour them, as it once did John; however, instead of locusts pork had been substituted on account of those wicked pagans. But Patrick did not so much as taste this food, for it was a sacrificial offering, and he remained unharmed and neither hungry nor thirsty. And as he slept that night, Satan attacked him violently, forming huge rocks and as it were already crushing his limbs; but he called on the name of Helias twice, the sun rose on him and with its beams it drove away all the gloom of darkness, and his strength was restored to him.

3   Many years later he again endured captivity at the hands of foreigners. And on the first night of his capture he was privileged to hear a divine voice prophesying to him: 'For two months you will be with them, that is to say, with your enemies.' And so it came about; on the sixtieth day the Lord delivered him from their hands, providing him and his companions with food and fire and dry weather every day until on the tenth day they reached human habitation.

4   And again a few years later he settled quietly as before in his home country with his kinsfolk, who welcomed him as a son, begging him never ever, after such trials and tribulations, to leave them for the rest of his life. But he refused to agree; and he was shown many visions there.

5   And he was thirty years old, as the apostle says, 'reaching perfect manhood, the measure of the age of the fulness of Christ.' (*Ephesians 4.13*) He set out to visit and pay his respects to the apostolic see, that is, to the head of all the churches in the whole world, in order to learn and understand the divine wisdom and holy mysteries to which God called him and to fulfil them; and so that he might preach and confer divine grace on foreign peoples by converting them to faith in Christ.

6   So he crossed the southern British sea, and beginning his journey through Gaul with the intention of eventually crossing the Alps, as he had resolved in his heart, he came on a very holy bishop, Germanus, who ruled in the city of Auxerre, the greatest lord in almost all of Gaul. He stayed with him for quite some time, just as Paul sat at the feet of Gamaliel; and in all humility, patience and obedience he learned, loved and treasured wholeheartedly knowledge, wisdom, purity and every benefit to soul and spirit, with great fear and love for God, in goodness and singleness of heart and chaste in body and spirit.

7   And when he had spent a considerable time there (some say forty
years, others thirty), that most faithful friend from time long past
called Victoricus, who had foretold everything to him before it
happened when he was in slavery in Ireland, visited him in a large
number of visions, telling him that the time was at hand for him to
come and fish with the net of the Gospel for the wild, barbarian
peoples whom God had sent him to teach; and there he was told in
a vision: 'The sons and daughters of the forest of Foclut are
calling you, etc.'

8   And so, when a suitable opportunity so directed, with God's
help to accompany him he set out on the journey which he had
already begun, to the work for which he had long been prepared -
the work, that is, of the Gospel. And Germanus sent an older man
with him, namely the priest Segitius, so that Patrick would have a
witness and companion, since he had not yet been consecrated to the
rank of bishop by the holy lord Germanus. For they were well aware
that Palladius, the archdeacon of Pope Celestine, the bishop of the
city of Rome who then held the apostolic see as forty-fifth in line
from St. Peter the apostle, that this Palladius had been consecrated and
sent to convert this island, lying as it does in frozen wintriness. But
God prevented him, because no one can receive anything from this
earth unless it has been given him from heaven. For these wild, un-
civilised people did not take kindly to his teaching, nor did he himself
want to spend time in a land which was not his own; he returned to
him who sent him. But on his return journey from here, after making
the first sea crossing and proceeding by land, he died in the land of
the British.

9   And so, when the word came of the death of St. Palladius in
Britain, since Palladius' disciples, Augustine, Benedict and the others,
returned to Ebmoria with the news of his death, Patrick and his
companions turned aside to a wonderful man, a very important bishop
called Amator, who lived nearby. And there St. Patrick, knowing what
was to happen to him, received the rank of bishop from the holy bishop
Amator, as also Auxilius and Iserninus and others received lesser
orders on the same day as St. Patrick was consecrated. They received
the blessings, everything was performed in the customary way, and
the following verse of the psalmist was also sung, especially appropriate
for Patrick: 'You are a priest for ever, in the manner of Melchisedek.'
(*Psalms 109.4*). Then in the name of the holy Trinity the venerable
traveller went on board the ship which had been prepared and reached
Britain; and as he made his way on foot he avoided all detours, except
for the ordinary business of travelling (for no one seeks the Lord by
idleness), and then he hurried across our sea with all speed and

a favourable wind.

10   Now in the days in which these events took place in the aforesaid area there was a certain king, the fierce heathen **emperor of the** barbarians, who reigned in Tara, which was the Irish capital. His name was Loegaire, the son of Niall and the ancestor of the royal house of almost the whole of this island. He had had wise men, wizards, soothsayers, enchanters and inventors of every black art who were able in their heathen, idolatrous way to know and foresee everything before it happened; two of them were favoured above the rest, their names being Lothroch, also called Lochru, and Lucetmael, also known as Ronal.

These two repeatedly foretold by their magical arts that there would come to be a certain foreign practice like a kingdom, with some strange and troublesome doctrine; a practice brought from afar across the seas, proclaimed by a few, adopted by many and respected by all; it would overthrow kingdoms, kill kings who resisted, win over great crowds, destroy all their gods, and after driving out all the resources of their art it would reign for ever and ever. They also identified and foretold the man who would bring and urge this practice in the following words, often repeated by them in a sort of verse form, especially in the two or three years preceding Patrick's arrival. This is how the verse ran; the sense is less than clear because of the different character of the language:

'Adze-head shall come, with his crook-headed staff and his house with a hole in its head. He shall chant blasphemy from his table, from the eastern part of his house, and all his household will answer him: 'So be it, so be it!'' (This can be expressed more clearly in our own language.) 'So when all these things happen, our kingdom, which is heathen, shall not stand.'

And this is just as it later turned out. For the worship of idols was wiped out on Patrick's arrival, and the catholic faith in Christ filled every corner of our land. So much for this topic; let us return to our subject.

11   So when the holy voyage had been successfully completed, the saint's ship, laden with wonderful religious treasures from across the sea, was brought, as to a suitable harbour, to the country of the Cualann, to a harbour in fact of some repute amongst us called Inverdee. And there it seemed to him that he could do no better than first to redeem himself; and so from there he set out for the north to that pagan Miliucc in whose household he had once been in captivity, bringing him a double ransom from slavery, an earthly and an heavenly one, so as to deliver from captivity the man to whom

he had previously been enslaved as a captive. He headed the ship's
bow towards the eastern island which is named after him to this
day, and from there he sailed on, leaving Brega and the Conaille
country and also the country of the Ulaid to his left, and finally put
into the sound called Brene (Strangford Lough). And he and those on
board with him landed at the mouth of the Slane, hid the ship and
went a little inland to rest there.

They were discovered by the swineherd of a man called Dichu, a
pagan but good at heart, who lived at the place where there is
now the barn named after Patrick (Saul). And the swineherd, thinking
that they were thieves and robbers, went off and informed his master
Dichu and brought him on them unknown to them. He had made up
his mind to kill them, but at the sight of St. Patrick's face the Lord
turned his thoughts to good. And Patrick preached the faith to him
and he believed Patrick there; and the saint rested there with him for
a few days.

But wishing to press on and visit the aforementioned Miliucc and
bring him his ransom and in that way convert him to faith in Christ,
he left the ship there with Dichu and proceeded to make his way on
land to the country of the Cruithne until he reached Mount Slemish.
It was from this mountain that long before, when he had been in
slavery as a captive there, he saw the angel Victoricus before his very
eyes ascend swift-footed into heaven and leave the imprint of his step
on the rock of the other mountain.

12   Now when Miliucc heard that his slave was coming back to visit
him and impose on him under duress, as it were, at the end of his
life a practice which he did not wish to accept, to avoid being
subjected to his slave and having his slave lord it over him, at the
devil's prompting he deliberately consigned himself to the flames
and, gathering around him all his goods and chattels, was burned to
death in the house in which he had previously lived as king.

Now as St. Patrick stood on the aforesaid spot on the south side
of Mount Slemish where, coming with such divine favour, he first
saw the district in which he had been a slave (to this day the place
is marked by a cross), there and then at the first glimpse of the district
he noticed before his eyes the king's burnt-out pyre. Dumbfounded
at this deed he uttered not a word for two or almost three hours; then
as he sighed and groaned and wept he spoke these words: 'I do not
know, but God knows; this man, this king who consigned himself to
the flames to avoid believing at the end of his life and serving the
eternal God, I do not know, but God knows, none of his sons shall
sit as king on the throne of his kingdom from one generation to the
next; moreover his descendants shall be slaves for ever.'

So saying, he prayed, armed himself with the sign of the cross and speedily retraced his steps back to the country of the Ulaid, and he came back to Magh Inis to Dichu: he stayed there for many days and went round the whole plain and chose and loved it, and the faith began to grow there.

13   Now during those days Easter approached, the first Passover which was celebrated to God's glory in this island Egypt of ours as it once was in Goshen. And they began to discuss where they should celebrate this first Easter among the heathen to whom God had sent them. Finally, when many proposals had been made on the subject, St. Patrick had the divinely inspired idea of celebrating this great festival of the Lord, as the chief of all festivals, in the great plain where there was the greatest kingdom of these peoples, the capital of all paganism and idolatry, so that here an invincible wedge could be driven into the head of all idolatry to prevent it ever again rising against the faith of Christ, with the hammer-blows of a resolute deed linked with faith, a hammer first wielded spiritually by St. Patrick and his followers; and so it turned out.

14   So the ship was carried down to the sea, and after taking leave of the good fellow Dichu in full faith and peace, they moved on from Magh Inis and leaving on their right hand for the future fulfilment of their ministry all that had previously, not inappropriately, been to their left, they came safe and sound to the harbour of the mouth of the Boyne (Drogheda). Leaving the ship there they went on foot to the aforesaid great plain, till finally towards evening they reached the Burial Ground of the men of Fiacc (Slane), which, as legend has it, was dug by the men, that is to say, the servants of Feccol Ferchertni, who was one of the nine magician prophets of Brega. And pitching his tent there, St. Patrick rendered with his followers the due paschal vows and sacrifice of praise to the most high God with all piety, in accordance with the prophet's word.

15   It happened that this was the year in which the heathen were accustomed to hold a festival of idolatry, with many enchantments, feats of magic and various other idolatrous superstitions, before a great gathering of the kings, governors, commanders, important personages and nobility of the people, not to mention the wizards, enchanters, soothsayers and devisers and teachers of every art and deceit, who were summoned to Loegaire, as once upon a time to king Nebuchadnezzar, at Tara, their Babylon; and they happened to be observing and celebrating that pagan festival on the same night as St. Patrick was celebrating Easter. They also had a custom, which was made known to all by proclamation, that if anyone in any part of the country, be it near or

far, lit a fire before one was kindled in the king's house, in the
palace of Tara, his soul would perish from among his people.

So St. Patrick, as he celebrated holy Easter, lit a divine fire,
very bright and blessed, and as it gleamed in the darkness it was
seen by almost all the inhabitants of the flat plain. So it came
about that it was seen from Tara, and everyone gazed in amazement
at the sight. The king called together the elders, councillors and
wizards and said to them: 'What is this? Who is it who has dared to
commit this sacrilege in my kingdom? Let him be put to death.'
And when all the elders and councillors replied to the king that they
did not know who had done it, the wizards replied: 'O king, live for
ever. This fire which we see and which was lit this night before one
was lit in your house, that is, in the palace of Tara, will never be
put out ever unless it is put out this night on which it has been lit;
and what is more, it will surpass all the fires of our practice; and he
who lit the fire and the coming kingdom by which it was lit this night
will overcome us all, and you, and will win over all the men of your
kingdom, and all kingdoms will yield to it, and it will fill all things
and reign for ever and ever.'

16   King Loegaire was deeply disturbed at these words, as was Herod of
old, and all the city of Tara with him. In reply he said: 'It will not be
so; no, we shall now go to see the end of the matter; we shall arrest
and put to death those who are committing such sacrilege against our
kingdom.' So yoking twenty-seven chariots as the tradition of the
gods demanded and taking these two wizards, Lucetmael and Lochru,
the best of all for this confrontation, Loegaire proceeded at the close
of that night from Tara to the Burial Ground of the men of Fiacc (Slane),
with his men and horses facing towards the left, that being the fitting
direction for them.

As they went, the wizards said to the king: 'O king, you shall not
go to the place where the fire has been lit, in case you afterwards do
obeisance to him that lit it; no, you will be outside, near at hand,
and he will be summoned to you, so that he will do obeisance to you
and it will be you who will be lord and master; and we and he shall
talk together in your sight, O king, and you will test us in this way.'
And the king replied: 'It is a good plan you have devised; I shall do
as you have said.' They reached the appointed place and dismounting
from their chariots and horses they did not enter the area immediately
surrounding the place where the fire had been lit, but sat down nearby.

17   St. Patrick was summoned to the king outside the place where
the fire had been lit. And the wizards said to their people: 'We shall
not rise to our feet at his approach; for whoever rises at his approach

will believe in him afterwards and do obeisance to him.' Finally
St. Patrick rose and seeing their many chariots and horses, he came
to them, rather appropriately singing with heart and voice this verse
of the psalmist: 'Some may go in chariots and some on horses, but
we shall walk in the name of our God.' (*Psalms 19.8*). They did not
rise at his approach; but just one, with God's aid, refused to obey the
wizard's words, namely Ercc, son of Daeg, whose relics are now venerated in the city called Slane, and he rose; and Patrick blessed him, and
he believed in the eternal God.

They then began to talk with one another, and one of the two
wizards, called Lochru, was insolent to the saint's face and had the
effrontery to disparage the catholic faith in the most arrogant terms.
St. Patrick glared fiercely at him as he spoke, as once Peter did with
Simon, and then, with strange power, he shouted aloud and con-
fidently addressed the Lord: 'O Lord, who can do all things and in
whose power all things lie, who sent me here, may this impious man
who blasphemes Your name be now carried up out of here and die
without delay.' At these words the wizard was carried up into the air
and then dropped outside from above; he fell head-first and crashed his
skull against a stone, was smashed to pieces and died before their eyes;
and the heathen were afraid.

18 The king with his followers was angry with Patrick at this, and he
determined to kill him and said: 'Lay hands on this fellow who is
destroying us.' Then seeing that the ungodly heathen were about to
rush him, St. Patrick rose and said in a clear voice: 'May God arise and
His enemies be scattered and those who hate Him flee from His face.'
And immediately darkness fell on them, and there was a horrible sort
of upheaval and the ungodly attacked one another, one rising up against
the other; and there was a great earthquake which locked their chariot-
axles together and drove them off violently, and the chariots and horses
careered at break-neck speed over the flat plain, until in the end only a
few of them escaped half-dead to the mountain Monduirn. And this
blow laid low seven times seven men at Patrick's curse before the king
and his elders until the king was left with only seven others; there
were himself and his wife and two kings and another four followers.
And they were very frightened.

And the queen came to Patrick and said to him: 'Sir, you are just
and powerful; do not destroy the king; for the king will come and bow
the knee and worship your Lord.' And the king came, compelled by
fear, and bowed the knee before the saint and pretended to worship
Him whom he did not want to worship. And after they had taken leave
of each other, the king, going a little way off, called St. Patrick over
on some pretext, with the intention of killing him some way or other.
But Patrick, aware of the wicked king's thoughts, first blessed his

companions (eight men and a boy) in the name of Jesus Christ, and
came to the king. The king counted them as they approached, and
immediately they disappeared clean out of the king's sight; the heathen
saw just eight deer with a fawn heading, as it were, for the wilds. And
king Loegaire, saddened, frightened and humiliated, returned at
dawn to Tara with the few survivors.

19   The following day, that is, Easter day, as the kings and princes
and wizards were lying at ease at Loegaire's house (for that was their
most important festival), as they ate and drank wine in Tara palace
and some talked while others thought about what had happened,
St. Patrick, accompanied by only five men, came to do battle and
speak for the holy faith in Tara before all the peoples, though the doors
were shut, just as we read about Christ.
      When he entered the banqueting-hall at Tara, not one of the number
rose at his approach except one person only, Dubthach maccu Lugil,
an excellent poet who had staying with him there at the time a certain
young poet called Fiacc, who was afterwards an admirable bishop and
whose relics are venerated at Sletty. As I said, this Dubthach was
the only one of the heathen to rise in honour of St. Patrick; and the
saint blessed him, and he was the first to believe in God that day, and
it was counted to him as righteousness. And when they saw Patrick,
he was invited by the heathen to eat his fill, so that they might test him
about things to come. But he, knowing what was to come, did not refuse
to eat.

20   Now while they were all feasting, that wizard Lucetmail, who had been
involved in the clash during the night, was also provoked that day by
his colleague's death to clash with St. Patrick; and to start off the contest,
as the others looked on he poured something from his own goblet into
Patrick's cup to test his reaction. And St. Patrick, seeing this kind of
test, blessed his cup in the sight of all, and the liquid turned into something like ice; and when the cup was turned upside down only the drop
which the wizard had poured in fell out. And he blessed the cup a second
time; the liquid returned to its natural state, and everyone was amazed.
      After a little while the wizard said: 'Let us perform signs on this
great plain.' And Patrick replied: 'What signs?' The wizard said: 'Let
us bring snow upon the land.' And Patrick said: 'I refuse to bring what
is contrary to God's will.' And the wizard said: 'I shall bring it in the
sight of all.' Then he began his magical spells and brought snow upon
the whole plain, deep enough to reach men's waists; and all saw and
were amazed. And the saint said: 'Right, we can see this; now take it
away.' He said: 'I cannot take it away before this time tomorrow.'
And the saint said: 'You can do evil, and not good. It is not like that
with me.' Then he gave his blessing over the whole plain round about,

and the snow disappeared quick as a flash, without any rain, clouds or wind. And the crowds shouted and were quite amazed and were filled with remorse.

Soon after, the wizard invoked demons and brought very thick darkness on the land as a sign; and they all muttered. And the saint said: 'Drive away the darkness.' But he could not. And the saint gave a blessing in prayer, and suddenly the darkness was driven away and the sun shone. And they all shouted aloud and gave thanks. Now when all this had taken place between the wizard and Patrick before the king's eyes, the king said to them: 'Throw your books into water, and we shall venerate the one whose books come out unscathed.' Patrick replied: 'I shall do so.' And the wizard said: 'I refuse to undergo a trial by water with this man; for he considers water to be his god.' (No doubt he had heard of baptism performed with water by Patrick.) And the king replied: 'Then pass them through fire.' And Patrick said: 'I am ready.' But the wizard refused, saying: 'This man worships in turn in alternate years now water, now fire as his god.' And the saint said: 'Not so. But you go yourself, and one of my boys will go with you into a house which stands apart and is closed up, and my garment will be about you, and yours about my boy, and you will then be burned together.'

This plan was settled upon, and the house was built for them, with one half made of green wood and the other of dry wood. And the wizard was sent into the house, into the green part of it, with Patrick's robe round him, and one of St. Patrick's boys, called Benignus, with the magic cloak into the dry part of the house. And so the house was closed up on the outside and was set on fire before the whole crowd. And it came about in that hour, as Patrick prayed, that the fire's flames consumed the wizard with the green half of the house, leaving only St. Patrick's robe untouched - it was not touched by the fire. Benignus, on the other hand, was more fortunate, as was the dry half of the house; the fire did not touch him, as is written of the three boys, nor was he distressed nor did it inflict any harm, except that the wizard's robe which had been about him was burned up, by the will of God.

The king was very angry with Patrick over the wizard's death and almost rushed at him with the intention of killing him. But God prevented him. For at Patrick's prayer and at his voice the wrath of God came down on the ungodly people and many of them perished. And St. Patrick said to the king: 'Unless you believe now, you will very soon die; for God's wrath will come down upon your head.' And the king was terrified and shaken at heart, and the whole city with him.

21   So king Loegaire assembled the elders and all his council and said to them: 'It is better for me to believe than to die.' And after taking counsel,

on his followers'instructions he believed that day and turned to the
eternal Lord God, and many others believed there. And St. Patrick
said to the king: 'Because you opposed my teaching and were a
stumbling-block to me, though the days of your reign be prolonged,
no one of your seed shall be king after you for ever.'

22   And St. Patrick, according to the Lord Jesus' command going and
teaching all nations and baptising them in the name of the Father and
of the Son and of the Holy Ghost, set out from Tara and preached, with
the Lord working with him and confirming his words with the following
signs.

The Brussels and Vienna MSS (B and C) begin book 2 after this point.

23   There was in Patrick's day a man in the country of the Ulaid called
Macuil Maccugreccae, and this man was very ungodly, a cruel tyrant,
with the result that he was called 'Cyclops'. He was evil in thought, im-
moderate in word, malevolent in deed, bitter in spirit, irate in temper,
vicious in body, savage in mind, pagan in way of life, a monster in
conscience; he plumbed such depths of ungodliness that one day as
he sat in a rugged spot high up on the hills, called *Druim Mocceuchach*,
where he played the tyrant every day, displaying the most heinous
signs of savagery and killing passing strangers with criminal brutality,
he saw St. Patrick, radiant with the bright light of faith and resplendent
with some wondrous diadem of heavenly glory, walking on his leisurely
way with unshakeable confidence in his doctrine, and he decided to
kill him too, saying to his followers: 'Look, here comes that deceiver
and corruptor of men who is in the habit of performing his tricks to
deceive men and mislead many. So let us go and test him, and we shall
find out whether that God in whom he boasts has any power.'
      And they tested the holy man in this way; they put in their midst
one of their number, who was perfectly well, lying with a blanket over
him and pretending to be mortally ill, to put the saint to the test in
such a deception, calling the saint a deceiver, his miracles tricks and his
prayers sorcery and spells. When St. Patrick approached with his disciples,
the heathen said to him: 'Look, one of us has been taken ill now; so come
and chant some of your religion's spells over him, in the hope that he
may be healed.' Now St. Patrick, knowing all their wiles and deceptions,
said firmly and fearlessly: 'No wonder he was taken ill.' His companions
uncovered the face of the man pretending to be ill and saw that he was

already dead. They were dumbfounded and astonished at such a miracle and said mournfully to one another: 'Truly this is a man of God; we did wrong to test him.'

St. Patrick turned to Macuil and said: 'Why did you want to test me?' And the cruel tyrant replied: 'I regret doing it; I shall do whatever you tell me and I surrender myself into the power of your most high God whom you preach.' And St. Patrick said: 'Then believe in my God the Lord Jesus Christ and confess your sins and be baptised in the name of the Father and of the Son and of the Holy Ghost.' And he was converted in that hour and believed in God eternal, and was baptised. And then Macuil went on to say: 'I confess to you, my holy lord Patrick, that I intended to kill you; so judge what punishment is due for such a horrible crime.'

And Patrick said: 'I cannot judge, but God will judge. But as for you, go away unarmed to the sea and cross quickly from this land of Ireland, taking nothing of your possessions with you except some poor little garment with which to cover your body, and tasting nothing and eating nothing of the produce of this island, and with the mark of your sin on your head; and when you reach the sea, shackle your feet together with iron fetters and throw the key into the sea, and put yourself into a boat made of one skin, without rudder and without oar, and be ready to go wherever wind and sea may take you; and whatever land Divine Providence may bring you to, dwell in it and carry out God's commandments there.' And Macuil said: 'I shall do as you say. But what shall we do about the dead man?' And Patrick said: 'He will live and get up without any pain.' And Patrick raised him in that hour, and he came back to life and health.

And Macuil journeyed from there as quickly as he could to the sea to the south of Magh Inis, in the unshakeable confidence of faith; he shackled himself on the shore, throwing the key into the sea as he had been instructed, and put out to sea in a boat. And a north wind blew on him and carried him southwards and cast him up on an island called *Evonia* (The Isle of Man). And he found there two most admirable men of shining faith and doctrine, who were the first to teach the Word of God and baptism in *Evonia*, and the islanders were converted by their teaching to the catholic faith; their names are Conindri and Rumili. Now when they saw the man with only one garment they were amazed and took pity on him and picked him up out of the sea, gladly welcoming him. So in the place where he had found spiritual fathers, in the land assigned to him by God, he trained body and soul in accordance with their rule and spent his whole lifetime with those two holy bishops until he was made their successor in the episcopate. This man is Macuil *dimane*, bishop and prelate of *Ardd Huimnonn*.

24   On another occasion, as St. Patrick was resting on the Lord's Day
on the sea-shore by the saltmarsh which is on the north side a short
distance away from Ox's Neck, he heard a noisy din coming from
pagans who were working on the Lord's Day making a rampart: so
Patrick called them over and forebade them to work on the Lord's
Day. But they did not comply with what the saint said; indeed they
laughed him to scorn. And St. Patrick said: '*Mudebrod*, however much
you work, may it get you nowhere.' So it was fulfilled. For the following night a great wind arose and stirred up the sea, and the storm
destroyed all the pagans' work, in accordance with the saint's words.

25   There was in the country of Airthir a rich and respected man
called Daire. Patrick asked him to give him some place for his religious
observances. And the rich man said to the saint: 'What place do you
want?' 'I want,' said the saint, 'you to give me that piece of high ground
which is called Willow Ridge, and I shall build a place there.' But he
refused to give the saint that high ground, but gave him another site on
lower ground, where there is now the Martyrs' Graveyard near Armagh,
and St. Patrick lived there with his followers.

But after some time there came a groom of Daire, bringing his remarkable horse to graze in the Christians' grassy meadow. And Patrick
was annoyed at the horse being brought in this way onto his ground and
said: 'Daire has acted stupidly in sending his brute beasts to disturb the
little ground that he gave to God.' But the groom like a deaf man did
not hear, and like a dumb man not opening his mouth he said nothing,
but let the horse loose there for the night and went away. But when the
groom came the following morning to see his horse, he found it already
dead. And returning home he sadly reported to his master: 'Look, that
Christian has killed your horse; the disturbance of his place annoyed him.'
And Daire said: 'Let him be killed too - go now and slay him.'

But as they went outside death fell on Daire quick as a flash. And
his wife said: 'This death is because of the Christian. Someone go
quickly and have his blessings brought back to us, and you will be saved;
and let those who have gone off to kill him be stopped and recalled.'
Two men went off to the Christian, and concealing what had actually
happened said to him: 'Look, Daire has been taken ill; let something be
brought to him from you, in the hope that he may be cured.' And
St. Patrick, knowing what had happened, said: 'To be sure.' And he
blessed some water and gave them it, saying: 'Go, sprinkle your horse
with this water and take it with you.' And they did so, and the horse
came back to life; and they took it with them, and Daire was cured by
the sprinkling of the holy water.

Afterwards Daire came to do honour to St. Patrick, bringing with him a
wonderful bronze bowl from across the sea, which could hold three *metretae*.

And Daire said to the saint: 'Look, take this bowl:' and Patrick said:
'*Grazacham*'. And Daire returned home and said: 'He is a fool who says
nothing better than *Grazacham* for a wonderful three *metretae* bowl.'
and to his servants he added: 'Go and bring us back our bowl.' They
went off and said to Patrick: 'We shall take the bowl.' And yet that time
too St. Patrick said: '*Grazacham*, take it:' and they took it. And Daire
asked his servants: 'What did the Christian say when you took the bowl
back?' They replied: 'He said *Grazacham* again.' Daire replied:
'*Grazacham* when you give it, *Grazacham* when you take it away: what
he says is so good - his bowl will be brought back to him with these
Grazachams'. And this time Daire came personally and brought the bowl
back to Patrick, saying to him: 'Here, keep your bowl. For you are a
firm, steadfast man. What is more, I give you, as far as it is mine to give,
that piece of ground which you once requested, and live there.' And that
is the city which is now called Armagh.

And they both went out, St. Patrick and Daire, to look at the wonderful offering and pleasing gift, and they climbed up to that high ground
and found a hind with her little fawn lying on the spot where now there
is the altar of the North church in Armagh. And Patrick's companions
wanted to take hold of the fawn and kill it, but the saint refused and
did not allow it; indeed the saint himself took the fawn, carrying it
on his shoulders; and the hind followed him like a very gentle, docile
ewe, till he had let the fawn go free in another wood lying to the
north side of Armagh, where the knowledgeable say there are some
signs remaining to this day of his miraculous power.

26   The knowledgeable tell of how a very hard and miserly man living
in Magh Inis reached such a criminal degree of stupidity and greed that
one day the fool forcibly drove away before St. Patrick's eyes, violently
and irresponsibly, the two oxen which drew Patrick's cart, while the
oxen were resting and grazing in his holding's pasture after their holy
work. And St. Patrick was angry with him and said with a curse: '*Mudebrod*,
you have done wrong. May neither you nor your descendants for ever have
any benefit from this field; from now on it will be useless.' And so it
came about. For a sea-flood came in that day, great enough to inundate
and cover the whole field, and, as the prophet says, 'fertile land was
turned into a salt-marsh because of the wickedness of the man who lived
on it.' (*Psalm 106.34*) This land has been sandy and infertile from the
day that St. Patrick cursed it right to the present day.

27   [And so, the Lord willing, I shall attempt to tell a few of the
numerous miracles of Patrick.] Once, when the whole of Britain was
frozen in the chill of unbelief, a certain king's remarkable daughter, called
Monesan, full of the help of the Holy Spirit, when someone asked for her

hand in marriage, did not consent; nor could she be forced to what she did not wish and what was a worse course, even when she had large quantities of water poured over her. For amid beatings and drenchings with water she used to ask her mother and her nurse whether they knew the maker of the disc by which all the world is given light, and when she received an answer which gave her to know that the sun's maker is He whose seat is heaven, when she was repeatedly pressed to be united to a husband in the marriage bond, she would reply, enlightened by the brightly shining counsel of the Holy Spirit: 'I shall certainly not do this.' For she looked for the maker of all creation through nature, following in this the example of the patriarch Abraham.

Her parents embarked on a plan given them by God; they had heard that a man Patrick was visited by the eternal God every seventh day, and so they travelled over to Ireland with their daughter and appealed to Patrick, whom they found after a laborious search. Patrick proceeded to ask these newcomers questions; then the travellers began to cry out and say: 'It is because of our daughter's ardent desire to see God that we have been induced and compelled to come to you.' Then Patrick, filled with the Holy Spirit, raised his voice and said to her: 'Well, do you believe in God?' She replied: 'I do.' Then he bathed her in the holy baptism of water and the Spirit. Very soon after she fell prostrate on the ground and delivered up her spirit into the angels' hands. She was buried at the spot where she died. Then Patrick prophesied that after twenty years her body would be removed with all honour from there to a neighbouring cell - as in fact happened later. And the relics of this woman from across the sea are venerated to this day.

28   I shall give a brief account of a miracle amazingly worked by the apostolic and Christ-like Patrick, our present subject; it is written that it happened almost uniquely to him when he was still in the flesh and to Stephen. One time when he was going off through the darkness to his usual spot to pray, he saw the usual heavenly signs: and wishing to test his very dear, loyal and holy boy, he said: 'My son, tell me, please, whether you perceive what I do.' Then the young lad, called Benignus, said without hesitation: 'Now I realise what you perceive; for I see the heavens open and the Son of God and His angels.' Then Patrick said: 'Now I perceive that you are my worthy successor.' And without delay they hurried on and came to the usual spot for prayer. And as they prayed in the middle of the river-bed, the lad said: 'I cannot endure the coldness of the water any longer;' for the water was too cold for him. Then Patrick told him to step down from the higher to a lower position; but he could not stand there for long either, for he protested that he felt the water hot; then, unable to bear standing there for any length of time, he clambered onto the bank.

29   I shall not pass over in silence an amazing feat of Patrick. News came to him of the quite iniquitous action of a certain British king called Coroticus, an ill-starred and cruel tyrant. He was a very great persecutor and murderer of Christians. Now Patrick tried to recall him to the way of truth by means of a letter; but he scoffed at its salutary warnings. When this was reported to Patrick, he prayed to the Lord and said: 'God, if it be possible, cast this traitor out from this present world and the world to come.' After only a short time had elapsed, Coroticus heard someone give a musical performance and sing that he would soon pass from his royal throne; and all his dearest friends took up the cry. Then, when he was in open court, he suddenly had the misfortune to take on the appearance of a little fox; he made off before his followers' eyes, and from that day and that hour, like a passing stream of water, he was never seen anywhere again.

NOTITIA DIGNITATUM
omnium tam civilium quam militarium, in partibus Orientis et Occidentis

The text depends on a transcript made in or about the tenth century. The transcript is lost, but copies made from it survive. The best and only available edition is by O. Seeck (1876, reprinted by Minerva GmbH, Frankfurt am Main, 1962). No critical commentary has yet appeared. The most recent and most comprehensive discussion is by A. H. M. Jones, *The Later Roman Empire* (1964) 3, 347 ff. The *Notitia* is the official list of all senior posts in the Empire, with their authorised establishments. It was probably drawn up in its present form about the year 395, and the western section was corrected up to the early 420s.

Several particulars which concern Britain require comment. First, the British entries were not deleted. In theory, the reason might be that fees went on being charged for the appointment of officers, who drew salaries for tasks which they could not undertake; but such an explanation is unevidenced and improbable, since numerous other discontinued appointments were removed from the lists. It is more likely that the British lists were retained because the Imperial government in the 420s regarded Honorius's instruction to the British to look after themselves as a temporary measure. They are therefore the official army-list for 406, the last year when the Imperial government in Italy controlled the army in Britain.

Other peculiarities of the British lists need explanation in the context of the order in which the *Notitia* arranges its information. The civilian offices raise few problems. The military lists distinguish field-army from frontier-forces. The ordering of the field-army is comparatively simple. The whole of the infantry and cavalry units are set down separately, in order of seniority. A third list gives their allocation to half-a-dozen regional *comites*, several of whom are also given establishments of their own later on in the *Notitia*; and some of these establishments also include frontier-units. Most of the *comites*, including the *Comes Britanniarum* (V 131; XXIX 4; Britanniae XXIX 1), command only units, detached from the field-army. The African *comites* have both frontier and field-army units, while the *Comes Litoris Saxonici per Britannias* (V 132; Britanniam XXVIII 1 and 12) alone is assigned frontier-troops only, and the *Comes Tractus Argentoratensis* is allocated no named units at all. Since the essential significance of the title *comes* is that its bearer commanded field-army units, it is probable that the British coastal *comes* had originally also commanded field-armies as well as frontier-units but had retained his title when they were posted away; and that the separate additional *comes Britanniarum* was a more recent creation. The elder Gratian, father of Valentinian, 'comes praefuit rei castrensis per Africam . . . multo postea pari potestate Britannum rexit exercitum' (Ammianus 30, 7). These words would equally fit the command of the coastal *comes*, attested in 367 (Ammianus 27, 8), and do not necessarily imply the existence of both *comites* so early.

The arrangement of the frontier-commands follows a precise and regular pattern, differentiated by clerical variations in their detailed presentation, two of which bear upon the history of the British army.

The *Notitia* lists the units in 28 frontier-commands, 14 in the east and 14 in the west. With two exceptions, each list has the units in order of seniority: first the cavalry, *cunei* before *equites*; then the *auxilia*, the *legiones*, the units styled *milites*, and the *classes* (fleets); at the end come the *alae* and *cohortes* which survived from the army of the early Empire, before Constantine. In the West, two units of foreign *gentes* are listed before the Roman infantry, and a late cohort and a legion head the lists of the *Tractus Armoricanus* and of the Britains, presumably because they were stationed at the headquarters of their respective *duces*. Some eight lists have additional units entered at the end, out of the order of seniority, presumably because they were late additions. One unit of *milites* in the Thebaid and two in Tripolitania appear out of their normal place; otherwise the precise order of seniority is observed without exception.

Rubrics (paragraph-headings) are given in the *Notitia*. They are of two kinds, those which distinguish provinces, and those which distinguish types of unit. Both are entered irregularly. Whenever a military command comprises troops in more than one civil province, each province is listed separately within that command, beginning with the most senior. There are eight such provinces, four each in East and West; for the Eastern commands, all or some of the rubrics are entered, but in the West they are not. In three of the four Western double commands, the provincial boundaries are well enough known, so that the headings Savia, Noricum and Raetia II may be restored under the commands of Pannonia II, Pannonia I and Raetia, since the locations given to troops in the second list are known to have lain in these provinces. In addition, the Raetia I lists enter separately an *ala* and two *cohortes*, second-century garrisons of the Danube downstream from Abusina (Eining) to Batavis (Passau), from an *ala* and four *cohortes* with Diocletianic titles upstream from Eining, where the river did not become the frontier until after the disasters of the mid-third century.

The eighth such command is that of the *Dux Britanniarum* (Oc. 40) where the list of second- and third-century *cohortes* and *alae* is followed by a *cuneus Sarmatarum* (presumably an upgrading of the earlier *ala Sarmatarum*) at Ribchester, a Diocletianic *ala* at Olenacum (possibly Lancaster, conceivably Ilkley), and an early-empire *cohors* at Brough-by-Bainbridge. Since *cunei* were the most senior of all frontier-units, and since in all other cases where the lists jump from a junior to a senior unit the reason is that they have begun to garrison a new province, it therefore follows that these three forts lay in a different province, possibly Valentia.

Apart from the old *alae* and *cohortes*, rubrics grouping kinds of unit are confined to the eastern Danubian lists, where they distinguish *Auxilia* or *Auxiliares* and *item legiones (ripenses)* in Scythia and Moesia II. The same categories and the same arrangement are also followed on the western Danube, but not elsewhere in the Empire. Evidently the compilers of the *Notitia* drew upon a Danubian list drawn up before the final division of the Empire, but the Western editors dispensed with its paragraph-headings.

These variants are purely scribal, but the variants prefixed to the lists of old *alae* and *cohortes* had a practical purpose. In all but the last of the Eastern commands, these units appear under the rubric 'et quae de minore laterculo emittuntur'. The reason is that in the East commissions for units entered in the *laterculum minus* (subsidiary schedule) were issued by the *quaestor*, those for units in the *laterculum maius* (main schedule) by the *primicerius* of the notaries; and, since considerable fees were charged for the commissions, each ministry keenly defended its rights. In the West, the old *alae* and *cohortes* of the *laterculum minus* remain in 10 of the 14 commands, listed in the same place and the same order and manner as in the East. But in the West, if any such distinction in the office responsible for commissions had existed, it had disappeared before the compilation of the *Notitia*, and the paragraph-heading no longer fulfilled a practical function. It is omitted from the lists for all the European western provinces, but retained, with variants, in Africa and Britain.

Three of the four African commands list simply *praepositi limitis* followed by a place-name, not recording the names of the individual units; but the *comes Tingitanae* command sets down the individual names of the *alae* and *cohortes* as well as their place of garrison. The *comites* of Africa and Tingitana retain the paragraph-heading *limitanei*, presumably because both also commanded field-army units, while the *duces* of Mauretania and Tripolitania leave it out. In Britain the *alae* and *cohortes* are prefixed with the rubric *item per lineam ualli*. They are set down in the same place, at the end of the list, as are all early Imperial auxiliary units throughout the *Notitia*; they differ from the western European commands, but resemble the East and Africa, in that they are prefixed by an appropriate rubric.

The main list of the *laterculum maius* units of the *Dux Britanniarum* is, like the rest of the *Notitia*, arranged in order of seniority. But the two other British lists, the *Comes Litoris Saxonici* and the *laterculum minus* list *per lineam ualli*, differ from all others in the *Notitia* in that the units are arranged in geographical order, instead of by seniority. Their similarity, together with their difference from the *Dux Britanniarum* and the rest of the frontier army, suggests that the two lists were drawn up on the same occasion. To suppose that the same anomaly occurred on two different occasions in Britain requires too great a trust in coincidence, and, since the third British list is of normal pattern, it cannot be regarded as a habit peculiar to British lists at all times.

The Saxon-Shore list gives some indication of the date of that occasion. It includes fortresses from the Wash to Southampton Water, but leaves out several whose archaeological traces remain, namely Lympne, Dover, Walton-on-the-Naze, and probably also Dunwich and Carisbrooke. These fortresses had presumably gone out of commission before the *Notitia* lists were set down. They are constructions of the late third or early fourth century, and the date when they ceased to be garrisoned is therefore probably the later fourth century. The occasion might be the reorganisation of the frontier by Count Theodosius in 368; possibly the work of Maximus about 381×383; conceivably that of Stilicho in 398, if the *Notitia* lists could themselves be so late. The evidence of the *Notitia* therefore argues that both the lists *Litoris Saxonici* and *per lineam ualli* were set down in their surviving form about the years 368/369.

At the end of four commands, units are added out of order, one *ala* each in Osrhoene and Pannonia II, two *classes* in Dacia Ripensis, a *legio* in Valeria. The Osrhoene *ala*, I Salutaris, is a late Imperial unit; the Pannonian *ala* and *legio* are named only from their station, as are the two *classes*. It is likely that all these units were added after the compilation of the lists.

A few cavalry-units are also named out of order, after the *legiones*, in the East. They comprise seven *alae*, of which four bear Theodosian names, and four units of fourth-century *equites*, one of which is Theodosian. All these units are the last entries in the *laterculum maius* in their respective commands, and are also probably additions to the original list.

In the west, a late *cohors* is placed before the *milites* in the *Tractus Armoricanus*, a *legio* before the *equites* and *numeri* in Britain. In both cases the unit is stationed at the headquarters of the *dux*, and may therefore claim seniority, in the compilation of these two lists.

PERIPLUS

Nennius 8. Nennius 7-9 epitomise a description of Britain. Britain is 800 miles long and 200 miles wide, with 28 *ciuitates* and 'innumerable' headlands and forts of stone and brick, and with three islands and many rivers. The text was probably of southern origin, since it distinguished the Thames and Severn from other rivers, as alone suitable for commercial navigation, but did not mention the Trent. Each of the three sections in Nennius is concluded by a separate sentence which looks like his own gloss: that Britain is inhabited by four nations, Gael, Pict, Saxon and British; that an 'ancient proverb' spoke of rulers of 'Britain with its three islands'; and that the British once ruled the whole island. The text is earlier than the mid-sixth century, since it was cited at length by Gildas (ch. 3) who also added his own glosses based on his own observation and his love of the British countryside; he mentioned the dimensions, the headlands, the 28 *ciuitates* and the forts, the rivers, and the trade of Thames and Severn, but not the islands. The dimensions come from Pliny, probably by way of Orosius (1, 2, 77). It is most unlikely that Nennius 8 is drawn from Gildas, since it does not use Gildas's language and lists the particulars in a different order, which is much closer than Gildas' to the form of known Roman geographical descriptions. The list of 28 cities contained in BL MS. Harley 3859 after the genealogies (Nennius 66a) including Cair Granth, Caer Peris, Caer Mincip, etc., is a medieval antiquarian attempt to supply names to the 28 *ciuitates* of Nennius 7.

PTOLEMY

The Geography, published *c.* 150, in Greek; the sections concerning Britain reproduced, with translation, *MHB*, xi ff.

The work is essentially a gazetteer to an atlas, giving references to most places by degrees of longitude and latitude.

The entries concerning Britain are mapped in the Ordnance Survey's *Map of Roman Britain*, p. 20.

THE 'TRIBAL HIDAGE'

Headings in square brackets are not in the text. Figures in round brackets are those of the Latin version where that differs from the English. Letters omitted in the text are placed in square brackets.

MYRCNA LANDES is	30,000	hyda thaer mon aerst Myrcna haet (ab eo loco ubi primum Mircheneland nominatur) (from the original Mercian territory)
[NORTH MERCIA]		[22,800 (22,200)]
W[r]ocen saetna	7,000	
Westerna eac swa (the same)	[7,000]	
Pec saetna	1,200	(600)
Elmed saetna	600	
Lindes farona	7,000	mid Haeth Feld lande
[SOUTH MERCIA]		[13,300 (12,600)]
[Middle Angles]		[5,700 (5,000)]
Suth Gyrwa	600	
North Gyrwa	600	
East Wixna	300	
West Wixna	600	(omit)
Spalda	600	
Wigesta	900	(800)
Herefinna (Hersinna)	1,200	(600?)
Sweordora	300	
Gifla	300	
Hicca	300	
[Wulfhere's annexations]		[7,600]
Wihtgara	600	
Nox gaga (Hex gaga)	5,000	
Oht gaga (Ocht gata, Gohraga)	2,000	thaet is 66,100 hyda [North and South Mercia 36,100 (34,800)]
[WEST MERCIA]		[19,000 (17,900)]
[South of the Wash-Avon watershed]		[16,300 (15,800)]
Hwinca (Hynica)	7,000	

Ciltern saetna	4,000	
Hendrica	3,500	(3,000)
Unecung[a]ga (Ynetunga)	1,200	
Aro saetna	600	
[North of the watershed]		[2,700] [(2,100)]
[East of Watling Street]		[1,500] [(900)]
Faerpinga	300	[Faerpinga] is in Middel Englu
Bilmiga	600	
iderigga eac swa (the same)	[600]	
[West of Watling Street]		[1,200]
East Willa	600	
West Willa	600	[MERCIA, total 55,100 (52,700)]
EAST ENGLE	30,000	
EAST SEXENE	7,000	
CANTWARENA	15,000	
SUTH SEXENA	7,000	(read Suth Sexe [septem hidas. West Sexe] chid)
WEST SEXENA		100,000 this ealles 242,700 (200,800 or 280,000) [REST OF ENGLAND, total 157,000] [MERCIAN EMPIRE, 212,100 209,000]

Text published BCS 297, 297a; *Liber Albus* (Rolls Series 2, 626); JBAA 40, 1884, 30.

The Figures

Bede, HE 3, 24 distinguished the territory of the South Mercians, granted by Penda to Peada in 653, from the North Mercians, separated by the Trent. The Trent is the frontier of sixth-century cemeteries; beyond it are a number of individual burials, including the very large number of barrows in Derbyshire and Staffordshire, none of which is known to be earlier than the seventh century. The Trent-border of the South Mercian sixth-century cemeteries extends from Burton to Newark. The 'Tribal Hidage' lists beyond the Trent three peoples with their own separate names, and one without, the *Westerna*; they presumably were seventh-century colonists, situated north-west of the South Mercians, and included many or most of the barrow-burials within their territory. Since Bede was concerned only with Peada's territory, he made no mention of West Mercia. The first groups of peoples and figures therefore represent *Mercia in 653*.

'Tribal Hidage'			Bede	
Westerna	7,000		North Mercians	7,000
[Middle Angles]	5,700	(5,000)	South Mercians	7,000
	127,000	(12,000)		12,000
[West Mercia]	19,000	17,900)		
	31,700	(29,900)		
Total, MYRCNA	30,000			
LANDES original territory				

(This total corresponds closely to the Latin texts' total.)

The text of the 'Tribal Hidage' adds the annexed peoples north of the Trent and inserts a total after North and South Mercia, which is correct, save that the compiler mistakenly added his total figure for original Mercia to the sum of its constituent elements.

The figures are:

Original North and South Mercia	12,700	(12,000)
Northern additions	15,800	(15,200)
Wulfhere's southern additions	7,600	(7,600)
	36,100	(34,800)
Original Mercian total, mistakenly added	30,000	–
	66,100	–

The original total is also wrongly incorporated in the grand total, to give 242,700 in place of 212,100. The discrepancy of 600 probably arises because a small West Mercian unit was omitted, or because one such unit was entered as 1,200 rather than 600.

All figures up to 1,200 are reckoned on a duodecimal long hundred basis of fractions of 12; larger figures are reckoned on a decimal basis of multiples of 1,000.

The English figure of 900 for the Wigesta is therefore more likely to be original than the Latin figure of 800, presumably a clerical error.

The curious figure for the Hersinna (Herstingas?) in the Latin text of *sex centum et duas hid* (variant corruption DCV, evidently from the common misreading of V for II) against the English 1,200, presumably derives from a misreading of 'two times six hundred'; and suggests that, throughout, the unit of Mercian reckoning was a grouping of 600 families or six hundreds.

The Geography

Of the 34 peoples mentioned, the approximate location of 30 is known, from Bede, the charters and other texts, or from surviving place-names. The Ordnance Survey's map of *Britain in the Dark Ages* summarises the evidence by printing the names. The known names are listed in strict geographical order; the four lost names cannot therefore be supposed to be exceptions.

Few of the printed names call for comment; the large *Wrocen saetna* are the population of the kingdom of Cynddylan of Wroxeter and the Wrekin, destroyed by Oswy in 655, and include the Lichfield-area, since Cynddylan appears to have ousted Morfael of Lichfield shortly before 655 (CLH 13, *Marwnad Cynddylan*, a tenth-century poem which incorporates stanzas from a much earlier poem, probably composed not long after the event). The South *Gyrwa* included Peterborough and Crowland, and perhaps surrounded *Sweordora*, to border on the *Elge* of Ely, included in East Anglia and therefore omitted from the Mercian territories in the 'Tribal Hidage'. But since the *Gyrwa* are named immediately after the *Lindes farona*, their northern territory probably bordered thereon, reaching up through the Lincolnshire Fens to the west of the *Spalda*.

The lost names are in two pairs. *Noxga ga* and *Ohtga ga* presumably lay between the Isle of Wight and the southern end of earlier southern Mercian (Middle Anglian) territory, in Hertfordshire. Place-names offer some pointers. No forms like 'Nocsga' are apparent, but traces of a people named 'Hecga' or 'Hecsga' favour the form of the name in the Latin text, *Hexga ga*. These names are difficult to distinguish from those derived from *haga*, hedge, *heah*, high, etc., but probably include *Hegcumb* and

Heglea in north-eastern Hampshire, near Farnham, and several other similar names (KCD 595, 1093; cf. index of places), and perhaps extend to Hedgerley near Gerrard's Cross in Buckinghamshire, 'Hycga's clearing' EPNS 238, and to Hexton in Hertfordshire, the *tun* of Heahstan, or at the stone of Hecga, EPNS 112. Names which suggest *Ohtga* lie farther east, with a boundary at *Ohha Haemes gemaera* near Bromley in Kent (KCD 700 [6, p. 243, appendix]), and may extend to Ockley south of Dorking and Ockham north-east of Guildford in Surrey, 'Occa's clearing' and 'homestead', EPNS 276, 143; they touch the 'Hecga' names about Farnham (KCD 1093, 624, etc.; index of places). The meaning and distribution of these names will be better understood when the Hampshire and Berkshire volumes of EPNS appear. At present it is possible to observe only that these names seem to congregate in the region where the 'Tribal Hidage' places the *Hexaga* and *Ohtga*.

The other pair of lost names is placed between the Chilterns and the *Aro saetna*, south of Stratford-on-Avon. The 'Hendrica' are presumably the *Hendre ga*, the 'nearer district' in and about northern Oxfordshire; the *Unecunga ga* beyond them are therefore placed in the difficult watershed-country between Banbury and Stratford, relatively poor in pagan cemeteries, where the colonisation of the early seventh century is marked by an unusually high proportion of the names which denote the settlements of humble cultivators, English or Welsh, *-cote* and *-ingtun*, and an unusually low proportion of those used by migrating peoples or substantial free farmers, *-ingas*, *-inga* and *-worth*. The name might derive from *unnyt* ('useless'), meaning 'unprofitable district' (cf. EPNE 2, 227), or might have some other less unflattering origin.

Date

The text gives a detailed census of the kingdom of Mercia and adds overall figures for the other kingdoms of the Southern English, over whom the Mercian monarchy asserted suzerainty. It excludes Northumbria.

In its present form it is later than Wulfhere's conquest of Wight in 661, earlier than the loss of Lindsey to Egfrith in 674/675 and than Wulfhere's cession of Wight and the Meonware to Sussex, some time before Wilfrid's arrival in Sussex in 680, before Wulfhere's death, and probably not long after 661. The early or mid-660s is a probable date.

But since Wulfhere's conquests are added in reverse geographical order to a Middle Anglian list which runs from north to south, the main body of Mercian figures may date from Penda's time. The inclusion of Elmet among the northern territories points to the same possibility; although nothing else is known of Mercian control of Elmet, or of the extent of territory regained by Wulfhere on his revolt, there is no reason to suppose that he retained authority so near to York for any length of time, if at all. On the other hand the *Wrocen saetna*, under their own British kings until 655, did not become Mercian until 658. The first version of this text may therefore have been drawn up *c.* 659/660, and it may therefore be that Wulfhere held Elmet for a short period. The compiler, however, started with an overall figure for the 'original Mercia', without the northern and southern additions. The figure is earlier than the present northern list and therefore suggests that a previous census was drawn up in Penda's time, when only the *Westerna* ranked as Mercians beyond the Trent. The listing of the West Mercian peoples in three separate provinces harks back to a very early stage in the formation of the kingdom: the compiler felt surprise, and the need of explanation, for the inclusion of *Faerpinga* (and the *Bilmiga* and *Widderiga*) of Northamptonshire and its borders among the West Mercians, though they were situated among the Middle Angles. The reason was clearly half-forgotten; it was already old, for the owners of the fifth-century cemeteries practised inhumation, in contrast with the cremation-cemeteries of the Middle Angles to their north, and the mixed cemeteries to their south. They had originally been a distinct group of peoples.

The list does not name London, or the various small peoples of the London region whose names are known; and it is not probable that London was included within the designation of *hexga* or *Ohtga*. London was therefore probably still regarded as part of the kingdom of Essex, and the text was therefore drawn up before the Mercians mastered the city; they did so at latest by the early years of Aethelred.

It is, however, possible that the round-figure totals for the southern kingdoms, other than Mercia, were added after Mercian suzerainty over the southern English was formally asserted by Aethelred.

Purpose

The text names hides, and groups them in hundreds. Bede, who gave the same figures for the North and South Mercians and the South Saxons, used 'terra familiarum', and the Old English translation renders his words as *folces*. The census enumerates families. It includes at least two regions, *Wrocen saetna* and Elmet, where, at the date of its compilation, almost the whole population was British speaking; and assigns to Wessex the enormous figure of 100,000, which, whether it is real or notional, plainly includes the British. The list therefore assesses total population, British as well as English.

A census by hides or families has two main purposes, either fiscal or military. It is scarcely probable that in the middle of the seventh century the recently subdued British were enrolled in English armies on the same basis as the English; although there is ample evidence for the participation of the forces of allied British kingdoms in Penda's campaigns, there is no hint anywhere that the British within the English kingdoms fought in English armies until they had been absorbed and had forgotten their distinct nationality. That degree of absorption is unlikely to have matured much before the middle of the eighth century. The census therefore is principally concerned with taxation.

Later fiscal assessments were concerned with the value and yield of land, rather than its crude population. A military assessment must stick close to real population, for, although 10 men may be made to pay the taxes of 20 men, they cannot be made to supply the manpower of twice their number.

Bede gave an assessment for Wight (HE, 4, 16) which is double that found in the Mercian census. His figure followed Ceadwalla's re-conquest when the king had been severely wounded, was furious with the islanders, and threatened to exterminate them and re-populate the island with his own direct subjects. It represents a doubling of their tribute rather than of their population.

Population

The census gives a total population of the Mercian empire of somewhat over 200,000 families, nearly half of them in Wessex. With a high infant and adolescent mortality rate, the number of children in each family is unlikely to have been less than three or four. The families are agricultural households, excluding domestic slaves, whose numbers were not likely to have been great. The total of persons listed is therefore not far short of a million. No figures are preserved for Northumbria, but its families must have numbered several score thousands. The figures therefore give a total of well over a million for the population of the English kingdoms.

WELSH POEMS

The principal poems are contained in four manuscripts, the Book of Taliesin, the Book of Aneirin, the Black Book of Carmarthen, the Red Book of Hergest. The texts were published in 1868, when the study of Old Welsh had barely begun, by W. F. Skene, *Four Ancient Books of Wales (FAB)*, and are there accompanied by hastily prepared translations whose English is comic rather than intelligible and has tended to bring the poems into disrepute. The principal modern editions are Sir Ifor Williams' *Canu Aneirin* (1938), *Canu Taliesin* (1960), *Canu Llywarch Hen* (1935), with A. O. H. Jarman's *Ymddiddan Myrddin a Thaliesin* (1951), all University of Wales Press, Cardiff. Sir Ifor Williams' three works select from the poems ascribed to these three poets those which appear to be of early composition. The complex linguistic evidence was summarised by Kenneth Jackson (*LHEB* 693): 'One can say that the Welsh language, in the form of primitive Welsh, had come into existence not by the first half but at any rate by the second half of the sixth century, and that the poems of Taliesin and Aneirin could have been composed in Welsh, not British, towards the end of that century. If so, they would be among the very first poets of the new language, the first to establish a tradition of Welsh, as distinct from British, poetry; and therefore the name of *Cynfeirdd*, "first" or "original" bards, traditionally given to the composers of this period, was very apt and justified.'

The texts of most of the other poems are available in J. G. Evans' *Black Book of Carmarthen*, facsimile edition, Oxford, 1888, and diplomatic edition, Pwllheli, 1906; *Book of Taliesin*, Llanbedrog, 1910; *Poetry from the Red Book of Hergest*, Llanbedrog, 1911, the Mabinogion and Brut texts therefrom being published separately (Oxford, 1887 and 1890). These books, and others, contain a considerable quantity of nature and other poetry not concerned with historical events, a selection of which has been published, without translation, by Kenneth Jackson, with the accurate but unhappy title of *Early Welsh Gnomic Poems*, Cardiff, 1935. Translations of various verses are to be found in Gwyn Williams' *The Burning Tree (TBT)* (parallel text), London (Faber), 1956, and *Presenting Welsh Poetry (PWP)* (translation alone), London (Faber), 1959; and in the opening pages of his *Introduction to Welsh Poetry*, London (Faber), 1953, of Sir Harold Bell's *Development of Welsh Poetry*, Oxford, 1936, and elsewhere. A number of texts appear in the *Oxford Book of Welsh Verse*, ed. Thomas Parry, 1962.